Student Guide

Book 1

THIRD EDITION

A TIMS® Curriculum
University of Illinois at Chicago

MATH TRAILBLAZERS®

Dedication

This book is dedicated to
the children and teachers who
let us see the magic in their classrooms
and to our families who wholeheartedly
supported us while we searched for
ways to make it happen.

The TIMS Project

UIC The University of Illinois at Chicago

The original edition was based on work supported by the National Science Foundation under grant No. MDR 9050226 and the University of Illinois at Chicago. Any opinions, findings, and conclusions or recommendations expressed in this publication are those of the authors and do not necessarily reflect the views of the granting agencies.

ISBN 978-0-7575-3480-5

Printed in the United States of America

1 2 3 4 5 6 7 8 9 10 11 10 09 08 07

Acknowledgments

Teaching Integrated Mathematics and Science (TIMS) Project Directors
Philip Wagreich, Principal Investigator
Joan L. Bieler
Howard Goldberg (emeritus)
Catherine Randall Kelso

Principal Investigators		
First Edition	Philip Wagreich Howard Goldberg	
Directors		
Third Edition	Joan L. Bieler	
Second Edition	Catherine Randall Kelso	
Senior Curriculum Developers		
First Edition	Janet Simpson Beissinger Joan L. Bieler Astrida Cirulis Marty Gartzman Howard Goldberg	Carol Inzerillo Andy Isaacs Catherine Randall Kelso Leona Peters Philip Wagreich
Curriculum Developers		
Third Edition	Janet Simpson Beissinger	Philip Wagreich
Second Edition	Lindy M. Chambers-Boucher Elizabeth Colligan Marty Gartzman Carol Inzerillo Catherine Randall Kelso	Jennifer Mundt Leimberer Georganne E. Marsh Leona Peters Philip Wagreich
First Edition	Janice C. Banasiak Lynne Beauprez Andy Carter Lindy M. Chambers-Boucher Kathryn Chval Diane Czerwinski	Jenny Knight Sandy Niemiera Janice Ozima Polly Tangora Paul Trafton
Illustrator		
	Kris Dresen	
Editorial and Production Staff		
Third Edition	Kathleen R. Anderson Lindy M. Chambers-Boucher	Anne Roby
Second Edition	Kathleen R. Anderson Ai-Ai C. Cojuangco Andrada Costoiu Erika Larson	Georganne E. Marsh Cosmina Menghes Anne Roby
First Edition	Glenda L. Genio-Terrado Mini Joseph Lynelle Morgenthaler	Sarah Nelson Biruté Petrauskas

Acknowledgments

TIMS Professional Developers

Barbara Crum
Catherine Ditto
Pamela Guyton
Cheryl Kneubuhler
Lisa Mackey
Linda Miceli

TIMS Director of Media Services

Henrique Cirne-Lima

TIMS Research Staff

Stacy Brown
Reality Canty
Catherine Ditto
Catherine Randall Kelso

TIMS Administrative Staff

Eve Ali Boles
Kathleen R. Anderson
Nida Khan
Enrique Puente
Alice VanSlyke

Research Consultant

First Edition

Andy Isaacs

Mathematics Education Consultant

First Edition

Paul Trafton

National Advisory Committee

First Edition

Carl Berger
Tom Berger
Hugh Burkhardt
Donald Chambers
Naomi Fisher
Glenda Lappan
Mary Lindquist
Eugene Maier
Lourdes Monteagudo
Elizabeth Phillips
Thomas Post

TIMS Project Staff

Table of Contents

Additional student pages may be found in the *Adventure Book* or the *Unit Resource Guide.*

Table of Contents

Additional student pages may be found in the *Adventure Book* or the *Unit Resource Guide.*

Letter to Parents

Dear Parents,

Math Trailblazers® is based on the ideas that mathematics is best learned through solving many different kinds of problems and that all children deserve a challenging mathematics curriculum. The program provides a careful balance of concepts and skills. Traditional arithmetic skills and procedures are covered through their repeated use in problems and through distributed practice. *Math Trailblazers,* however, offers much more. Students using this program will become proficient problem solvers, will know when and how to apply the mathematics they have learned, and will be able to clearly communicate their mathematical knowledge. Computation, measurement, geometry, data collection and analysis, estimation, graphing, patterns and relationships, mental arithmetic, and simple algebraic ideas are all an integral part of the curriculum. They will see connections between the mathematics learned in school and the mathematics used in everyday life. And, they will enjoy and value the work they do in mathematics.

The *Student Guide* is only one component of *Math Trailblazers.* Additional material and lessons are contained in the *Adventure Book* and in the teacher's *Unit Resource Guides.* If you have questions about the program, we encourage you to speak with your child's teacher.

This curriculum was built around national recommendations for improving mathematics instruction in American schools and the research that supported those recommendations. The first edition was extensively tested with thousands of children in dozens of classrooms over five years of development. In preparing the second and third editions, we have benefited from the comments and suggestions of hundreds of teachers and children who have used the curriculum. *Math Trailblazers* reflects our view of a complete and well-balanced mathematics program that will prepare children for the 21st century—a world in which mathematical skills will be important in most occupations and mathematical reasoning will be essential for acting as an informed citizen in a democratic society. We hope that you enjoy this exciting approach to learning mathematics and that you watch your child's mathematical abilities grow throughout the year.

Philip Wagreich

Philip Wagreich
Professor, Department of Mathematics, Statistics, and Computer Science
Director, Institute for Mathematics and Science Education
Teaching Integrated Mathematics and Science (TIMS) Project
University of Illinois at Chicago

Unit 1

Welcome to Second Grade

	Student Guide	Adventure Book	Unit Resource Guide*
Lesson 1			
Hundreds of Coins			●
Lesson 2			
Birth Months	●		
Lesson 3			
Animals Galore	●		
Lesson 4			
Animal Trading Cards	●		
Lesson 5			
Addition Facts Strategies	●		

***Unit Resource Guide* pages are from the teacher materials.**

Name ______________________ Date ____________

Ms. Carter's Class

Ms. Carter's class recorded information in a data table. The students used the data table to make a graph. Use the graph to answer questions on the following page.

Birth Months

B	C
JANUARY	4
FEBRUARY	2
MARCH	6
APRIL	0
MAY	1
JUNE	2
JULY	2
AUGUST	4
SEPTEMBER	0
OCTOBER	2
NOVEMBER	3
DECEMBER	3

HAPPY BI

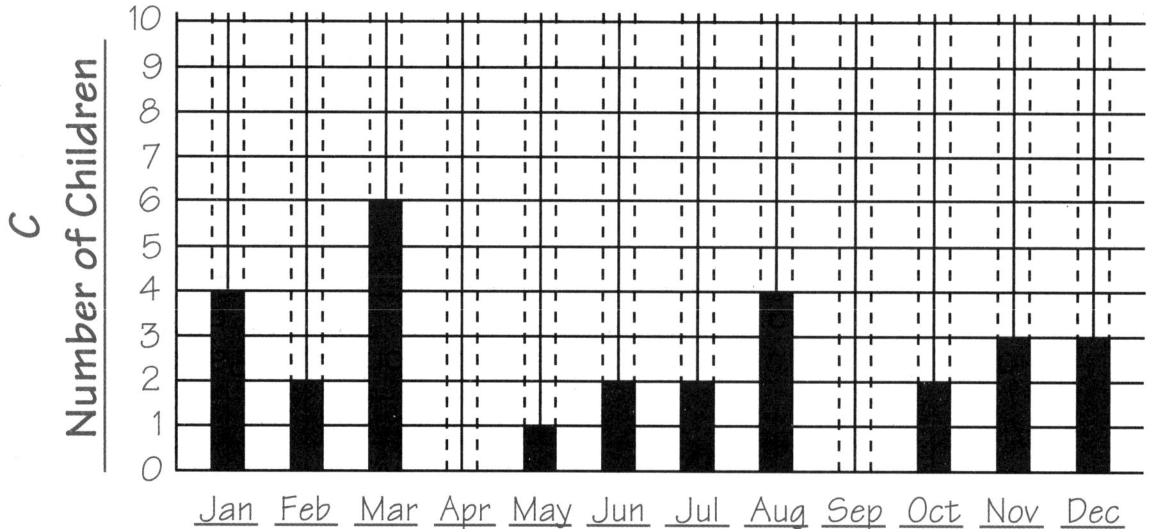

Birth Month

B

Name ______________________ Date ____________

1. What is the most common birth month in Ms. Carter's class? How do you know?

____

____

2. What is the least common birth month? ____________

3. How many children have birthdays in August? ________

4. Which months have the same number of birthdays?

____

5. How many students are in Ms. Carter's class? ________

6. Is Ms. Carter's class larger, smaller, or the same size as your class? How do you know?

____

____

7. How is your class graph different from Ms. Carter's class graph?

____

____

____

Name ______________________ Date ______________

Animal Problems

1. Five kittens are playing with a ball of string. Three more kittens are eating.

   How many kittens are in the litter? ________

2. A pod of whales has 3 males and 9 females.

   How many whales are in the pod? ________

3. A pig has 9 piglets in her litter. She already fed five of the piglets. The rest are hungry.

   How many hungry piglets are there? ________

4. A pack of wolves has 5 adults and 8 pups.

   How many wolves live in this pack? ________

5. There was a herd of elephants. Three baby elephants were born. Now there are seven elephants.

   How many elephants were in the herd to start? ________

6. There were 11 chattering monkeys. Four fell asleep.

   How many monkeys are still chattering? ________

7. There were 12 toads sitting near the pond. Some jumped away. Four toads are still sitting near the pond.

   How many toads jumped away? ________

Name ______________________ Date ____________

Animal Trading Cards

Pod of Whales **4¢**

Troop of Monkeys **5¢**

Pride of Lions **6¢**

Parliament of Owls **7¢**

Pod of Whales **4¢**

Troop of Monkeys **5¢**

Pride of Lions **6¢**

Parliament of Owls **7¢**

Pod of Whales **4¢**

Troop of Monkeys **5¢**

Pride of Lions **6¢**

Parliament of Owls **7¢**

Name ______________________ Date ______________

Animal Trading Cards Problems

4¢ 5¢ 6¢ 7¢

Solve the problems. Write a number sentence for each.

1. Michelle bought a Pod of Whales card and a Pride of Lions card. How much did she spend?

   ____

2. Loni bought two Pride of Lions cards. How much did she spend?

   ____

3. Katrina spent 13¢. Which cards did she buy?

   ____

4. Freddie spent 9¢. Which cards did he buy?

   ____

5. Tony bought a Pod of Whales card, a Troop of Monkeys card, and a Parliament of Owls card. How much did he spend?

   ____

Name ______________________ Date ______________

More Animal Trading Cards Problems

Work with your partner to solve the problems. Write number sentences for each. Use your trading cards and counters to help you.

4¢ 5¢ 6¢ 7¢

1. Lowell bought 2 cards. Both of the cards are the same. He spent 14¢. What did he buy?

____

2. Bill bought 2 different cards. He spent 11¢. What did he buy? Find 2 solutions.

____

3. Martina had 10¢. She bought 2 cards. She can buy more than one of each card. What can she buy? Find 2 solutions.

____

4. Sara bought 3 cards and spent 15¢. She can buy more than one of each card. What can she buy? Find 2 solutions.

____

Name ______________________ Date ______________

Different Solutions

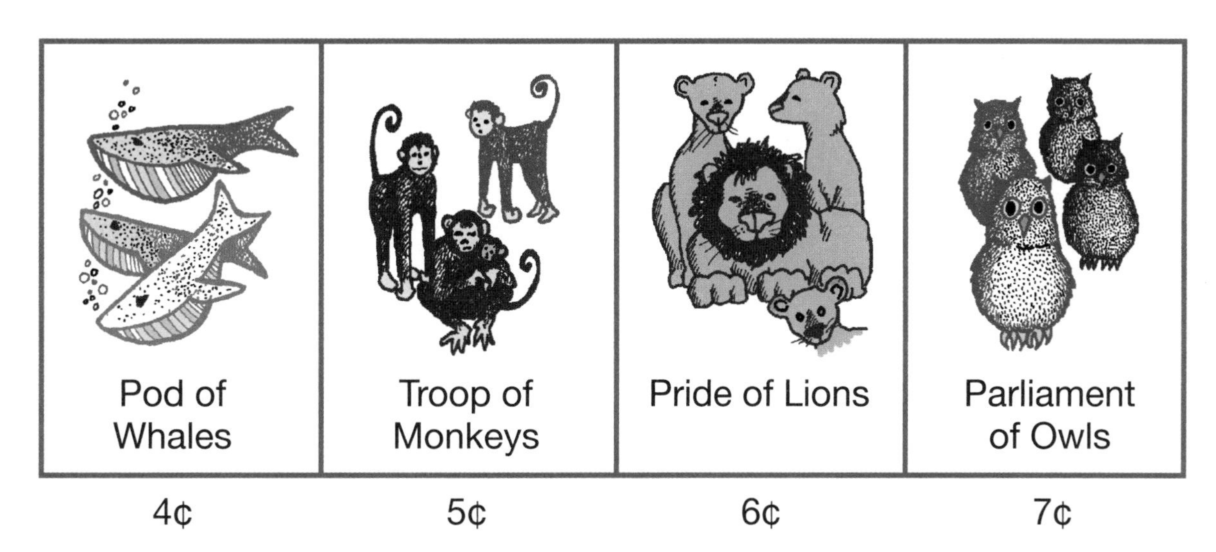

Shanta bought three cards and spent 18¢. She can buy more than one of each card. What cards can she buy? Find as many solutions as you can. Write a number sentence for each. Use counters and your trading cards to help you.

____

____

____

Name ________________________ Date ______________

Empty Ten Frames

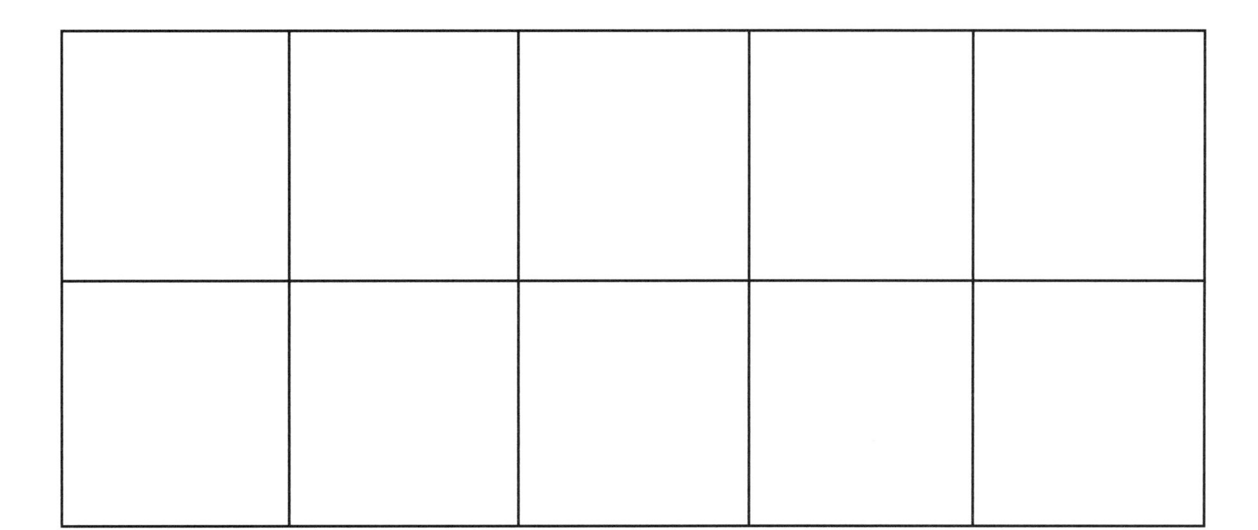

Name ______________________ Date ______________

Ten Frames

Cut along the dotted lines.

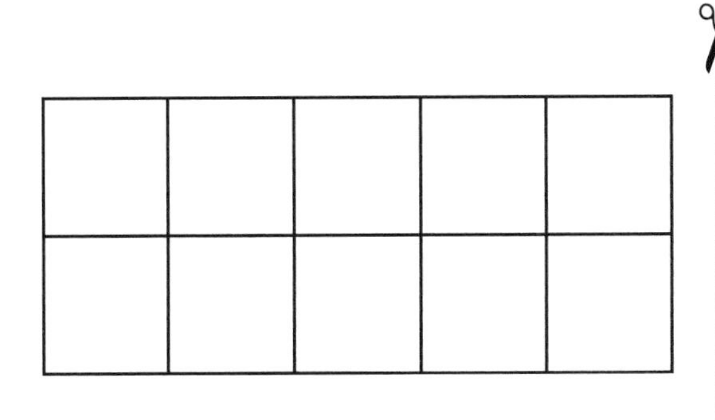

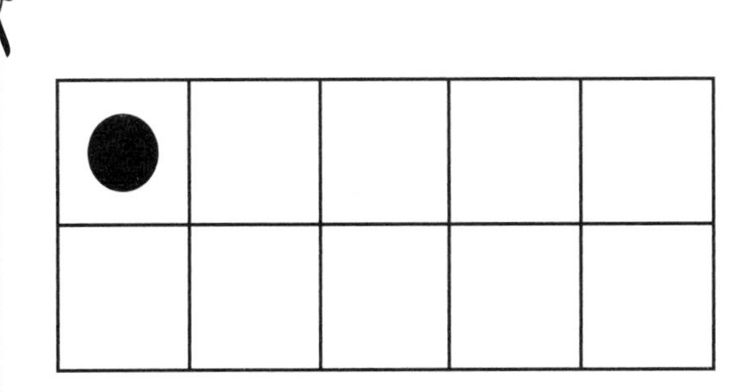

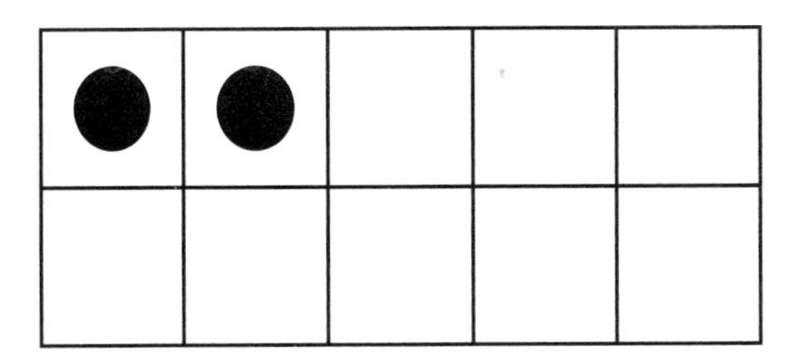

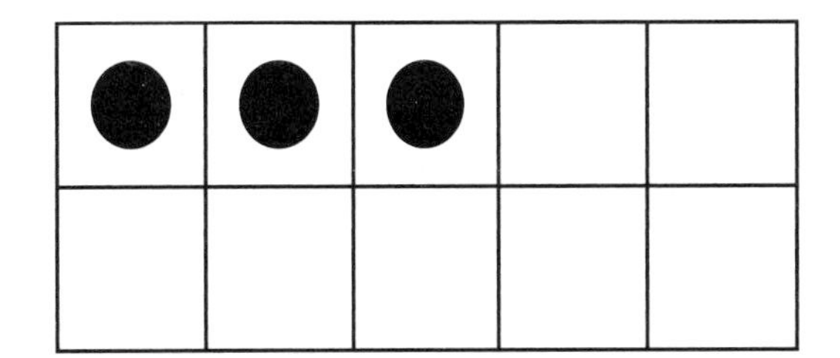

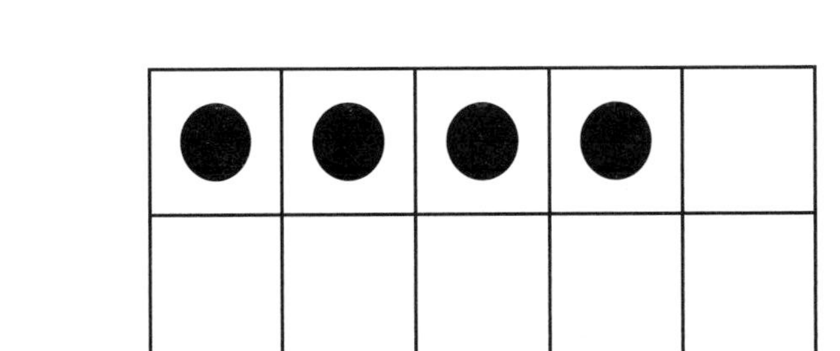

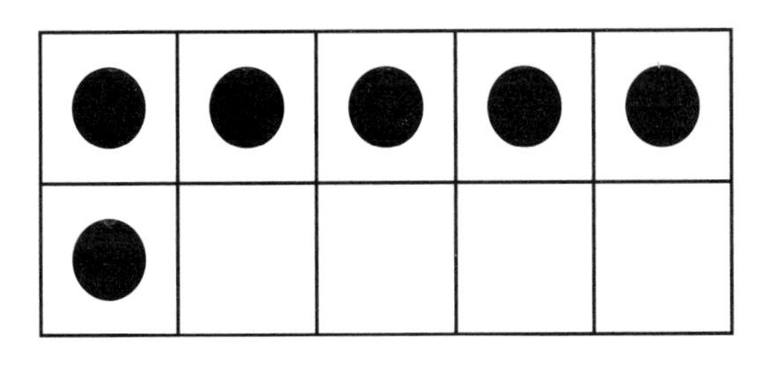

Name ____________________ Date ____________

Cut along the dotted lines.

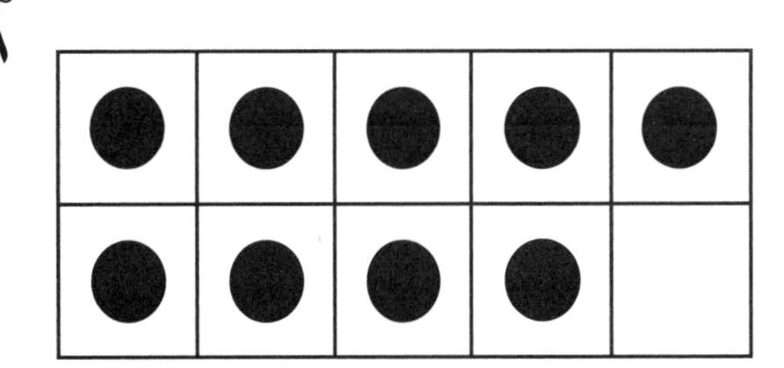

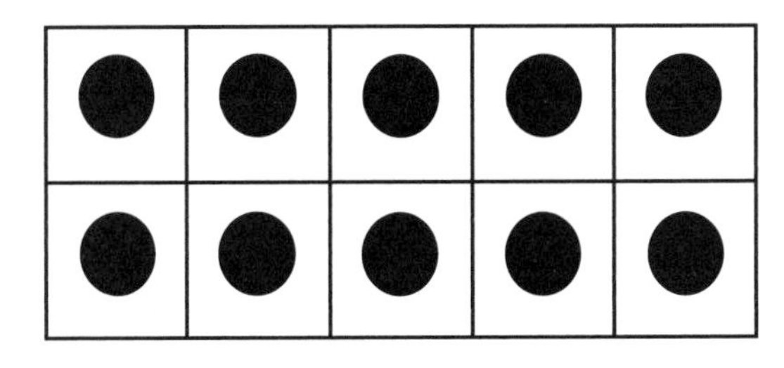

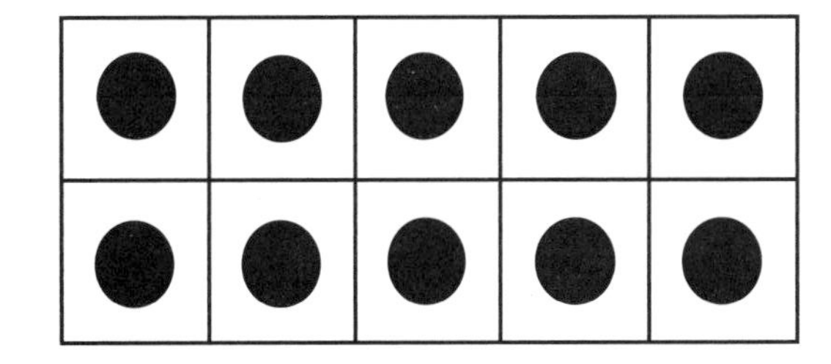

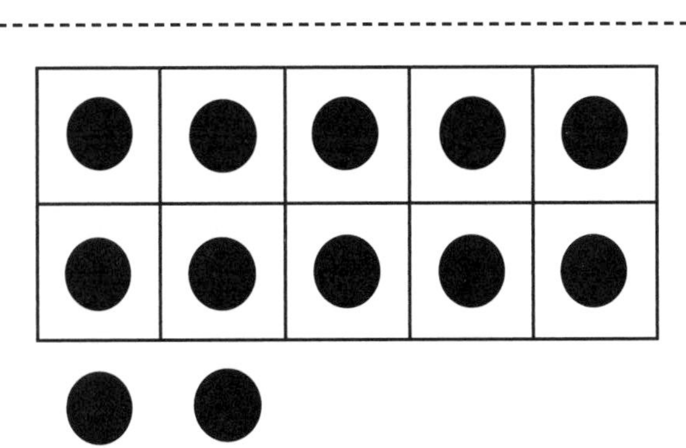

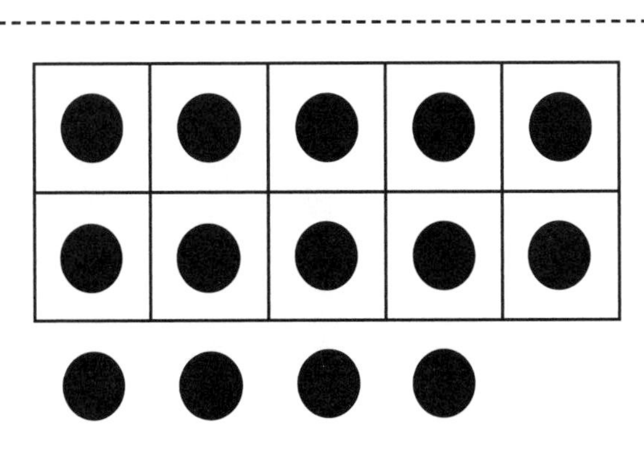

Name ______________________ Date ______________

Double Ten Frames

Write two number sentences for each pair of ten frames.

Two number sentences for the ten frames on the right are

$9 + 6 = 15$
and
$5 + 5 + 4 + 1 = 15$

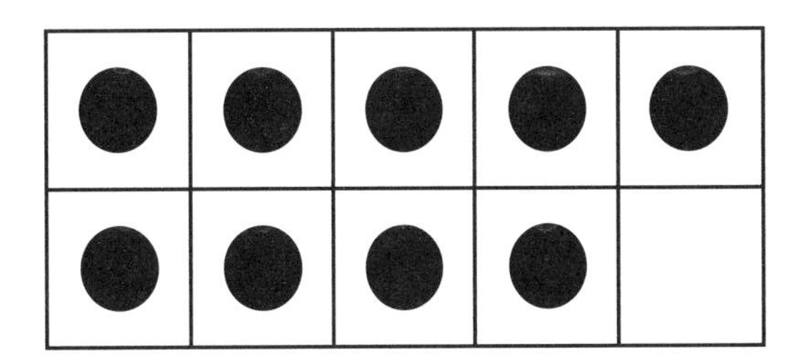

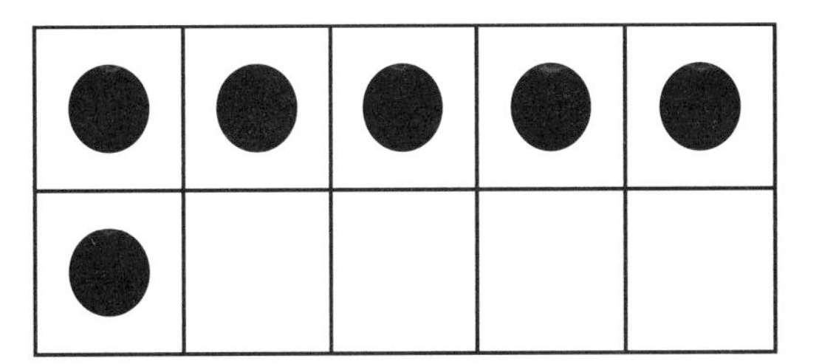

1. ______________________

____

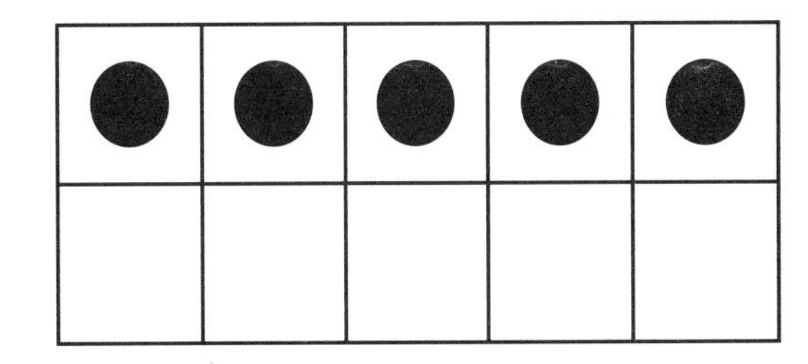

2. ______________________

____

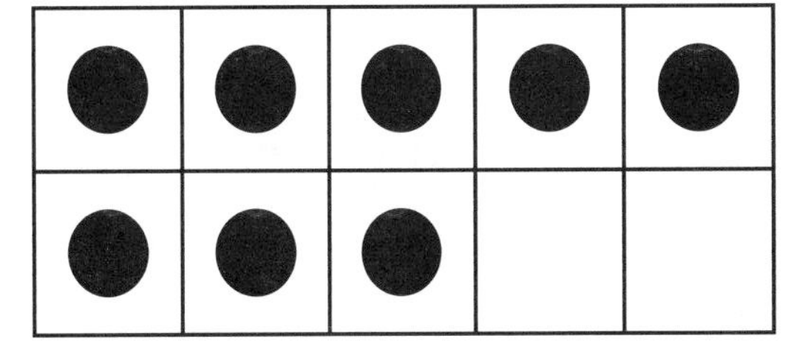

Name ______________________ Date ______________

3. ______________________

____

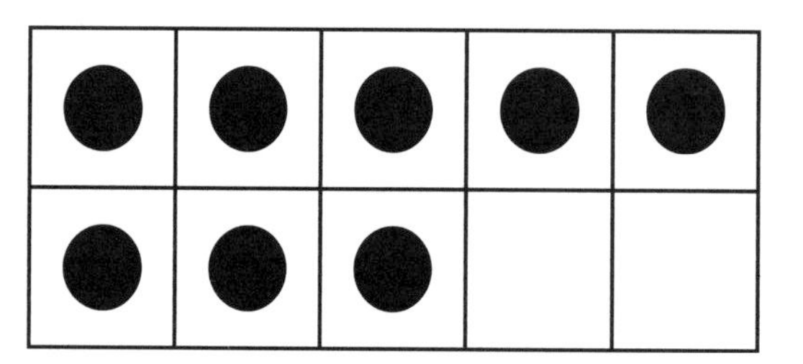

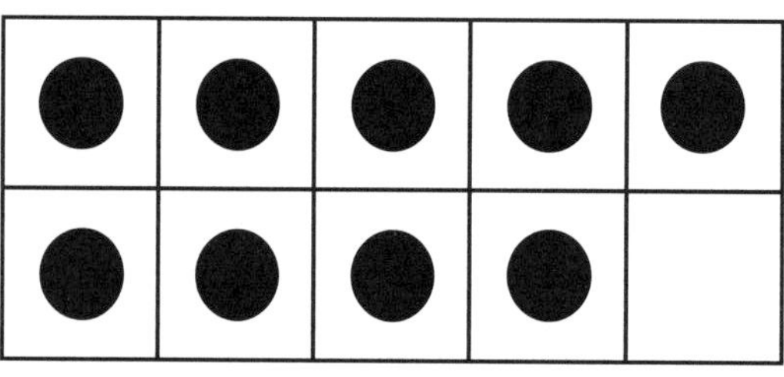

4. ______________________

____

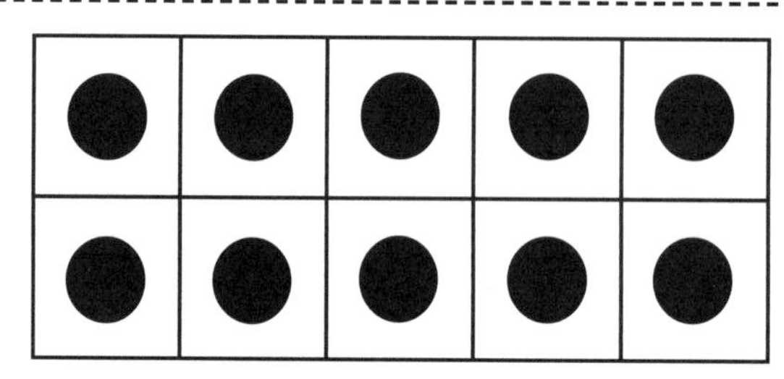

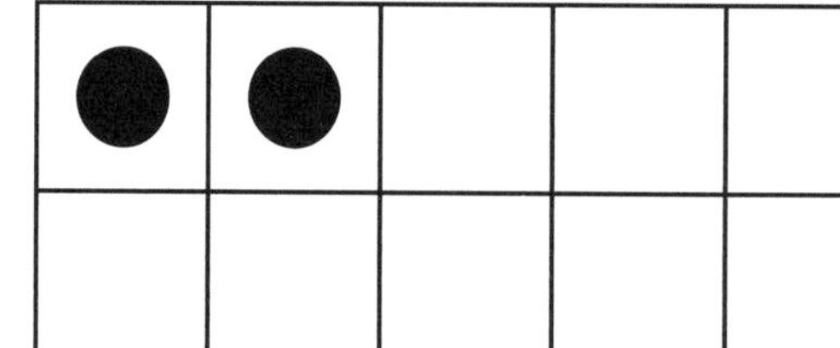

5. ______________________

____

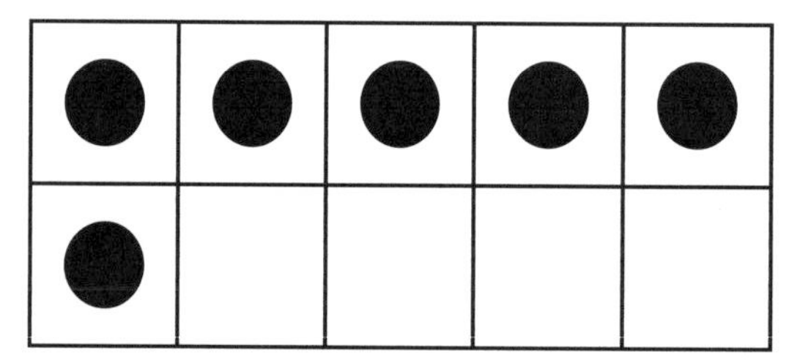

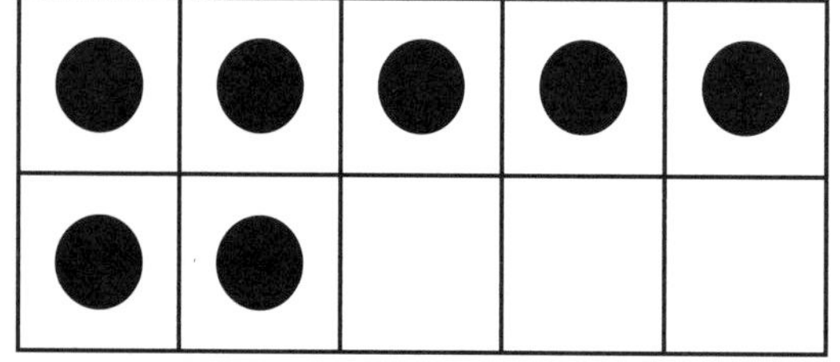

Unit 2

Exploring Numbers

	Student Guide	Adventure Book	Unit Resource Guide*
Lesson 1			
Tile Designs	●		
Lesson 2			
Exploring the *200 Chart*	●		
Lesson 3			
My Favorite	●		
Lesson 4			
Check It Out!		●	
Lesson 5			
Subtraction Facts	●		
Lesson 6			
Cover Up	●		
Lesson 7			
The Zoo Gift Shop	●		

******Unit Resource Guide*** **pages are from the teacher materials.**

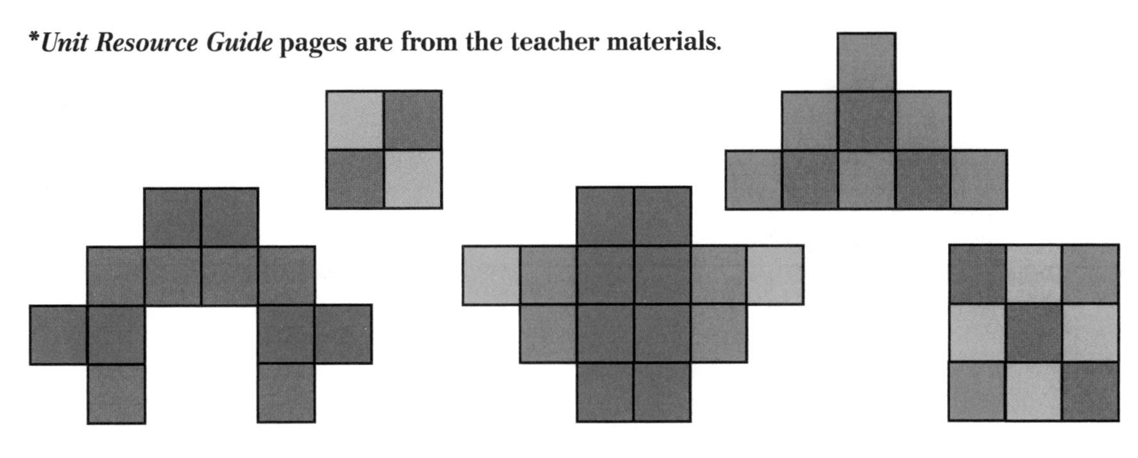

Name ______________________ Date ______________

What's My Number Sentence?

Write two number sentences for each tile design.

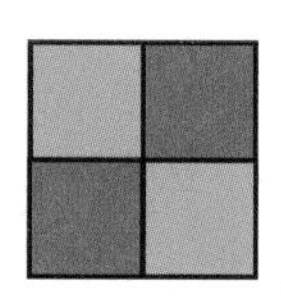

1. A. ______________________

   B. ______________________

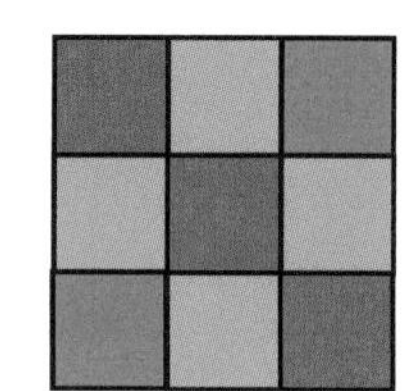

2. A. ______________________

   B. ______________________

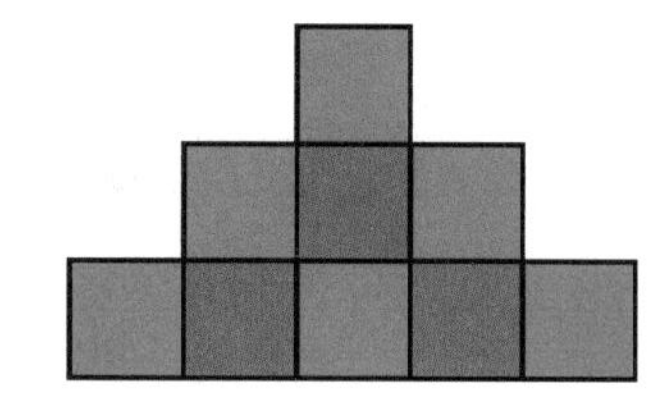

3. A. ______________________

   B. ______________________

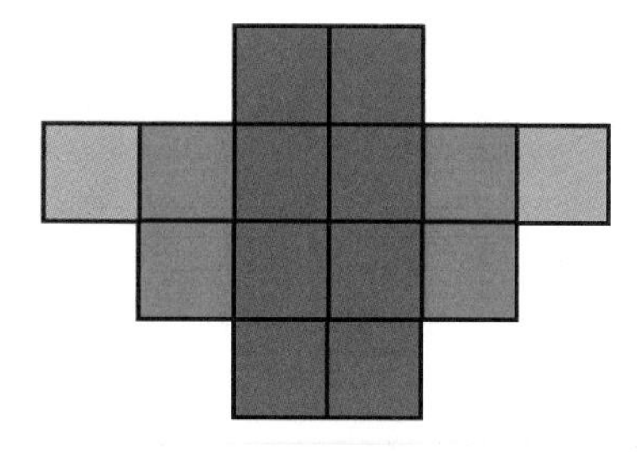

4. A. ______________________

   B. ______________________

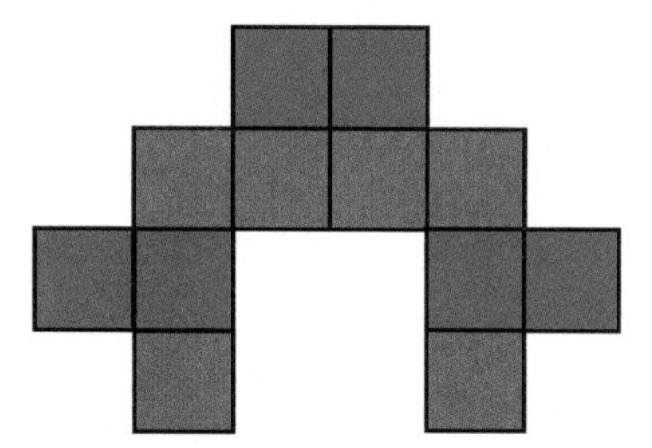

5. A. ______________________

   B. ______________________

Name ______________________ Date ______________

Make Your Own Tile Design

Use tiles to make a design on the grid. Color the squares to record your design. Write your number sentences on a separate sheet of paper.

Name ______________________ Date ______________

Miko's Tile Design

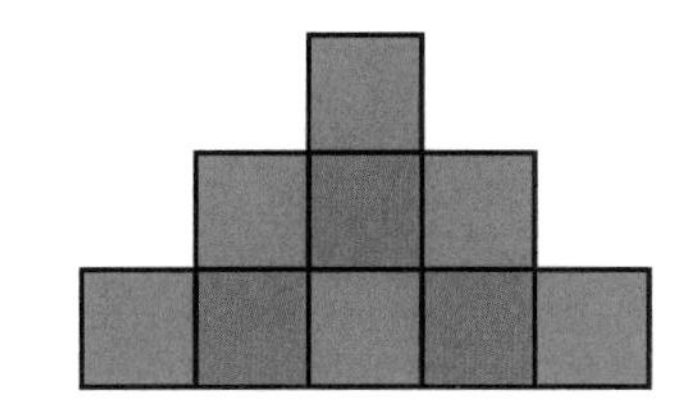

Miko made this design using color tiles. She wrote this number sentence to describe it.
1 + 2 + 3 + 2 + 1 = 9

Amy wrote another number sentence for the same design. 1 + 3 + 5 = 9

1. Tell how Miko and Amy were looking at the design when they wrote these number sentences.

   Miko

   ____

   ____

   Amy

   ____

   ____

2. Write a different number sentence to describe Miko's design.

   ____

Name ______________________ Date ______________

Building a 200 Chart

1	2	3	4		6	7		9	10
11	12			15		17			20
		23					28	29	
31			34						40
		43				47			
	52						58		
				65		67			
	72				76				
81									90
91			94					99	100
			104					109	
	112					117			
					126			129	
131				135					140
	142						148		
			154		156				
	162							169	
171				175					
181			184			187			
191	192	193	194	195	196	197	198	199	200

Name ______________________ Date ______________

200 Chart

1	2	3	4	5	6	7	8	9	10
11	12	13	14	15	16	17	18	19	20
21	22	23	24	25	26	27	28	29	30
31	32	33	34	35	36	37	38	39	40
41	42	43	44	45	46	47	48	49	50
51	52	53	54	55	56	57	58	59	60
61	62	63	64	65	66	67	68	69	70
71	72	73	74	75	76	77	78	79	80
81	82	83	84	85	86	87	88	89	90
91	92	93	94	95	96	97	98	99	100
101	102	103	104	105	106	107	108	109	110
111	112	113	114	115	116	117	118	119	120
121	122	123	124	125	126	127	128	129	130
131	132	133	134	135	136	137	138	139	140
141	142	143	144	145	146	147	148	149	150
151	152	153	154	155	156	157	158	159	160
161	162	163	164	165	166	167	168	169	170
171	172	173	174	175	176	177	178	179	180
181	182	183	184	185	186	187	188	189	190
191	192	193	194	195	196	197	198	199	200

Name ______________________ Date ______________

Moving on the 200 Chart

Players

This is a game for two players.

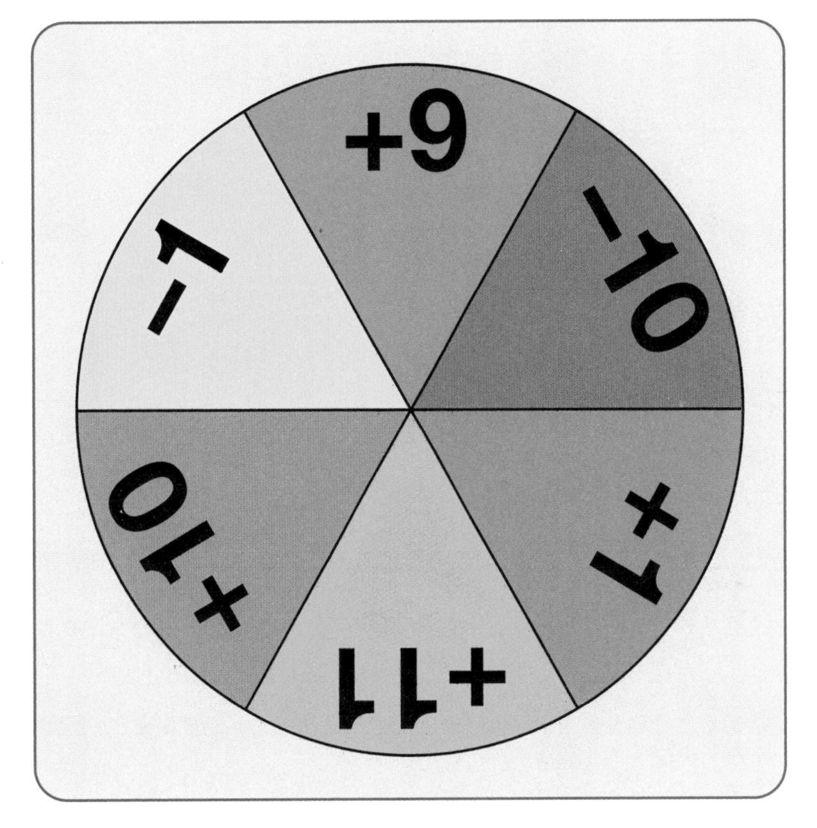

Materials

- a spinner
- a scorecard
- a *200 Chart*

Rules

1. Begin at 50 on the *200 Chart*.
2. Spin, and do what the spinner tells you.
3. Record your spin and your new number on your scorecard.
4. Take turns until your scorecard is full.
5. The player with the larger number at the end wins!

Name ________________________ Date ______________

Moving on the 200 Chart Scorecard

Player 1 ______________

Start with 50.

Spin	New Number

Player 2 ______________

Start with 50.

Spin	New Number

Name ______________________ Date ______________

Spin and Add Playing Board

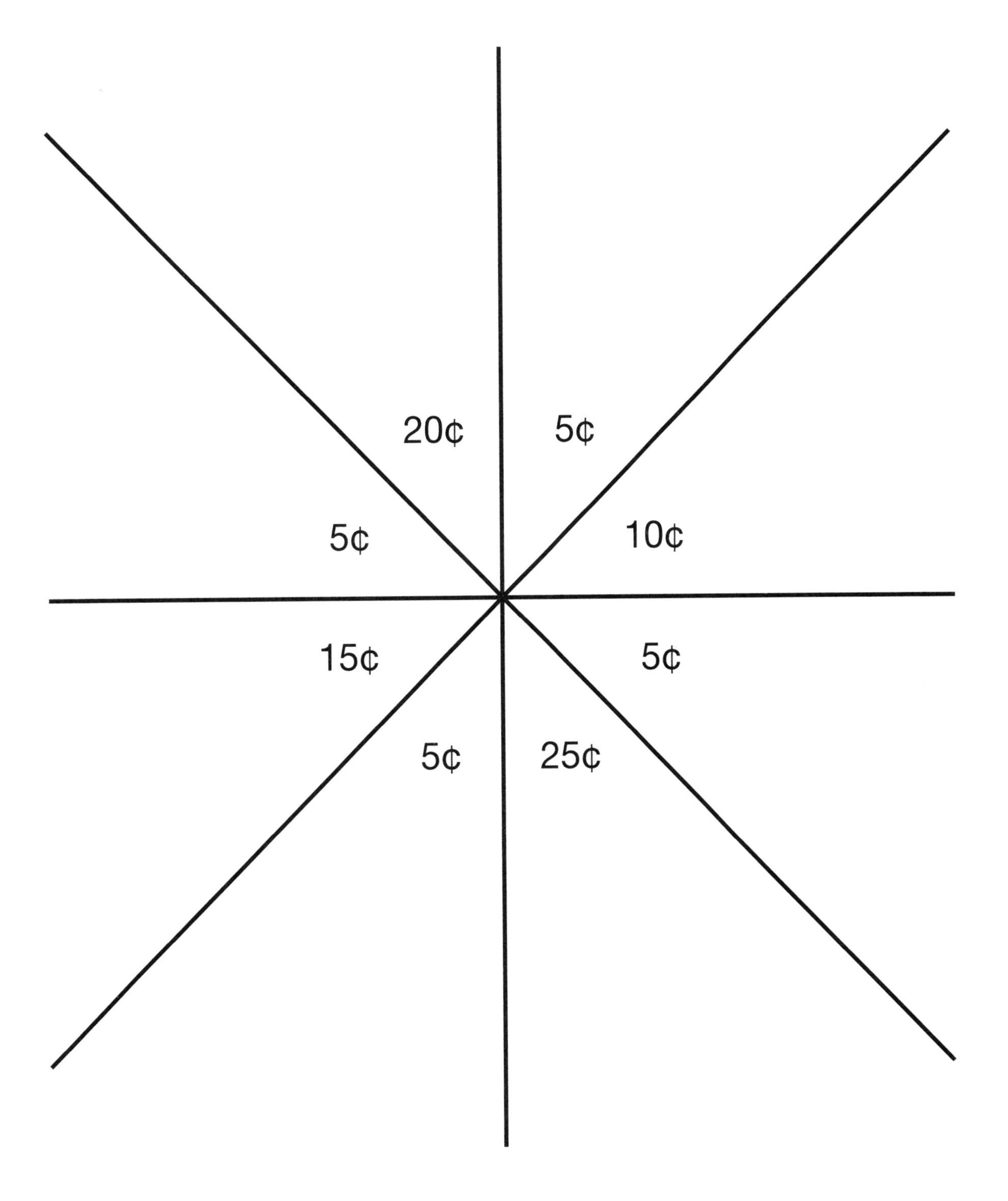

Name ________________________________ Date ________________

Spin and Add Score Sheet

Players

This is a game for two players.

Materials

- *Spin and Add Playing Board*
- *Spin and Add Score Sheet*

Rules

Each player records the sum of three spins for each round. Players 1 and 2 compare their sums. The player with the higher sum gets one point. If the sums are the same, both players get one point.

	Sums		Points	
	Player 1	Player 2	Player 1	Player 2
Round 1				
Round 2				
Round 3				
Round 4				
Round 5				
Round 6				
Round 7				

Total ________ ________

Name ______________________ Date ______________

Missing 200 Chart Numbers

Dear Family Member:

Your child has been working on patterns and relationships using a *200 Chart*. Refer to the *200 Chart* on the back of this page. Each square below represents a section of the chart with numbers missing. As shown in the example, a move up decreases the number by ten, down increases it by ten, left decreases it by one, and right increases it by one.

Thank you for your cooperation.

Pieces of the *200 Chart* are shown below. Fill in the missing numbers.

1	2	3
11	**12**	13
21	**22**	23

Example

	27	
		38

	73	
	83	

78		
	89	

Name ______________________ Date ______________

200 Chart

1	2	3	4	5	6	7	8	9	10
11	12	13	14	15	16	17	18	19	20
21	22	23	24	25	26	27	28	29	30
31	32	33	34	35	36	37	38	39	40
41	42	43	44	45	46	47	48	49	50
51	52	53	54	55	56	57	58	59	60
61	62	63	64	65	66	67	68	69	70
71	72	73	74	75	76	77	78	79	80
81	82	83	84	85	86	87	88	89	90
91	92	93	94	95	96	97	98	99	100
101	102	103	104	105	106	107	108	109	110
111	112	113	114	115	116	117	118	119	120
121	122	123	124	125	126	127	128	129	130
131	132	133	134	135	136	137	138	139	140
141	142	143	144	145	146	147	148	149	150
151	152	153	154	155	156	157	158	159	160
161	162	163	164	165	166	167	168	169	170
171	172	173	174	175	176	177	178	179	180
181	182	183	184	185	186	187	188	189	190
191	192	193	194	195	196	197	198	199	200

Name ______________________ Date ______________

Mr. Hart's Class

Mr. Hart's class collected data on their favorite taco. Here is their data table and graph.

Our Favorite Taco

T Type of Taco	*C* Number of Children
Steak	6
Chicken	7
Beef	9
Pork	0
Veggie	2
Avocado	3

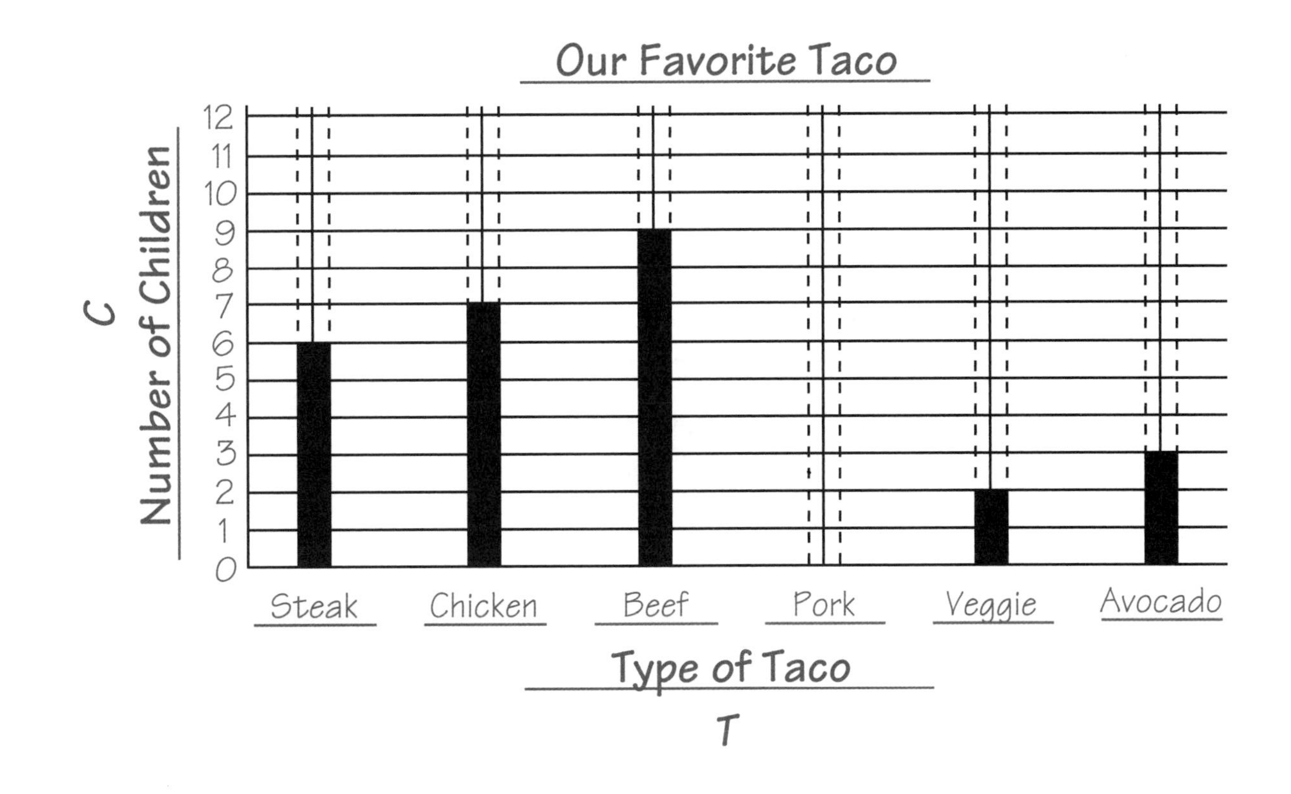

Name ______________________ Date ______________

1. What is the most popular type of taco in Mr. Hart's class? How do you know?

____

____

2. What type of taco is the least favorite?

____

3. How many children chose chicken tacos as their favorite?

____

4. How many students are in Mr. Hart's class?

____

5. Mr. Hart ordered one taco for each of his students. The veggie and the avocado tacos were placed in a blue bag. The steak tacos were put in a yellow bag. Which bag has more tacos? How many more?

____

6. Two new students were added to the class. Joe and Anita both chose pork tacos as their favorite. Change the data table and graph to show Joe and Anita's data.

Name ______________________ Date ______________

Fun at the Carnival

Dear Family Member:

You can help your child solve these problems by reading the problems with him or her, providing counters (such as beans or pennies) to use as problem-solving tools, and asking your child to share his or her strategies.

Thank you.

Solve these problems in the way that works best for you. Write number sentences for each question.

1. Frank and Luis saved money to go to the carnival. Frank saved $15 and Luis saved $19. How much more money did Luis save than Frank?

2. Both boys waited in line for a ride on the Scrambler. Frank waited 11 minutes. Luis waited 5 minutes. How much longer did Frank have to wait than Luis?

3. Frank had 15 tickets. He used 6 tickets to ride the roller coaster. How many tickets did Frank have left?

4. Luis bought 2 hotdogs for $1 each. He gave the hotdog seller $5. How much money did Luis get back in change?

5. Frank bought a box of Chocos Candies. The box had 14 candies. He gave 7 candies to Luis. How many candies did Frank have left?

Name ______________________________ Date ________________

More Fun at the Carnival

Solve these problems in the way that works best for you. Use ten frames, counters, or connecting cubes. Write number sentences for Questions 1–4.

1. Luis tried to win a bear for his sister at the ring toss. He tossed 12 rings. Five rings landed on the mark. How many rings missed the mark?

2. It takes 9 rings on the mark to win a bear. How many more rings does Luis need to win a bear?

3. Luis and Frank wanted to take a ride together. The ride cost 6 tickets for each boy. Frank had 4 tickets. Luis had 5 tickets. How many more tickets did they need to go on the ride?

4. When they got home, Luis and Frank counted their money. Luis had 7 nickels. Frank had 13 nickels. How many more nickels did Frank have than Luis?

5. What is the value of each boy's money?

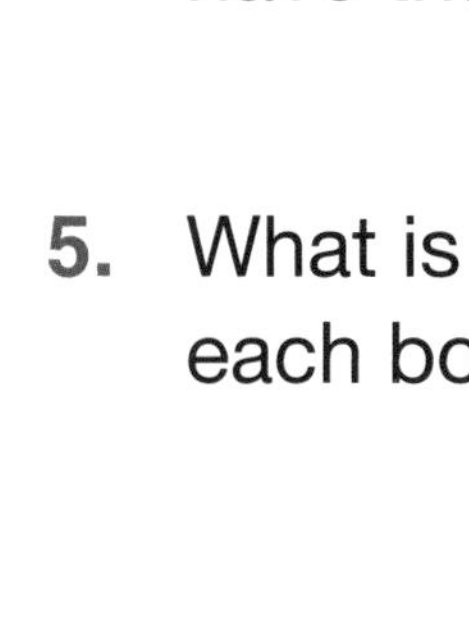

Name ______________________________ Date ________________

Cover Up

Total Number of Beans ________________

Write number sentences to describe each "cover up" problem.

Number of Beans Showing	Number of Beans Covered	Number Sentence

Name ______________________ Date ______________

Zoo Gift Shop Animal Figures

Fill in prices for the animals below.

Name ______________________ Date ______________

Garage Sale Problems

Dear Family Member:

In class, your child is learning about money. Help him or her solve the garage sale problems below. Your child should write a number sentence to describe each problem. For example, a comic book and two baseball cards cost $8 + 3 + 3 = 14¢$.

Thank you for your cooperation.

Solve the problems below. Write a number sentence for each.

doll clothes for 14¢ a set	comic books for 8¢ each
stickers for 4¢ each	markers for 9¢ each
lemonade for 7¢ a cup	baseball cards for 3¢ each

1. How much for one sticker and one comic book?

____

2. How much for a marker and a cup of lemonade?

____

3. How much change from a dime do you get if you buy a sticker and a baseball card?

____

4. You have 35¢. What can you buy? Write two number sentences.

____

____

Unit 3

Buttons: A Baseline Assessment Unit

	Student Guide	Adventure Book	Unit Resource Guide*
Lesson 1			
All Sorts of Buttons	●		
Lesson 2			
A Handful of Buttons	●		
Lesson 3			
Button Sizer	●		
Lesson 4			
Addition with Triangle Flash Cards	●		
Lesson 5			
Button Solutions	●		
Lesson 6			
Button Place Value	●		

******Unit Resource Guide*** **pages are from the teacher materials.**

Name ______________________ Date ____________

All Sorts of Buttons 1

List as many ways as you can to sort the buttons.

___

___

___

___

___

___

___

___

___

___

___

___

___

Name ______________________ Date ______________

All Sorts of Buttons 2

Draw

How I sorted my buttons:

Name ______________________________ Date ____________________

How Would You Sort Them?

Sort the following buttons. Describe how you sorted them below.

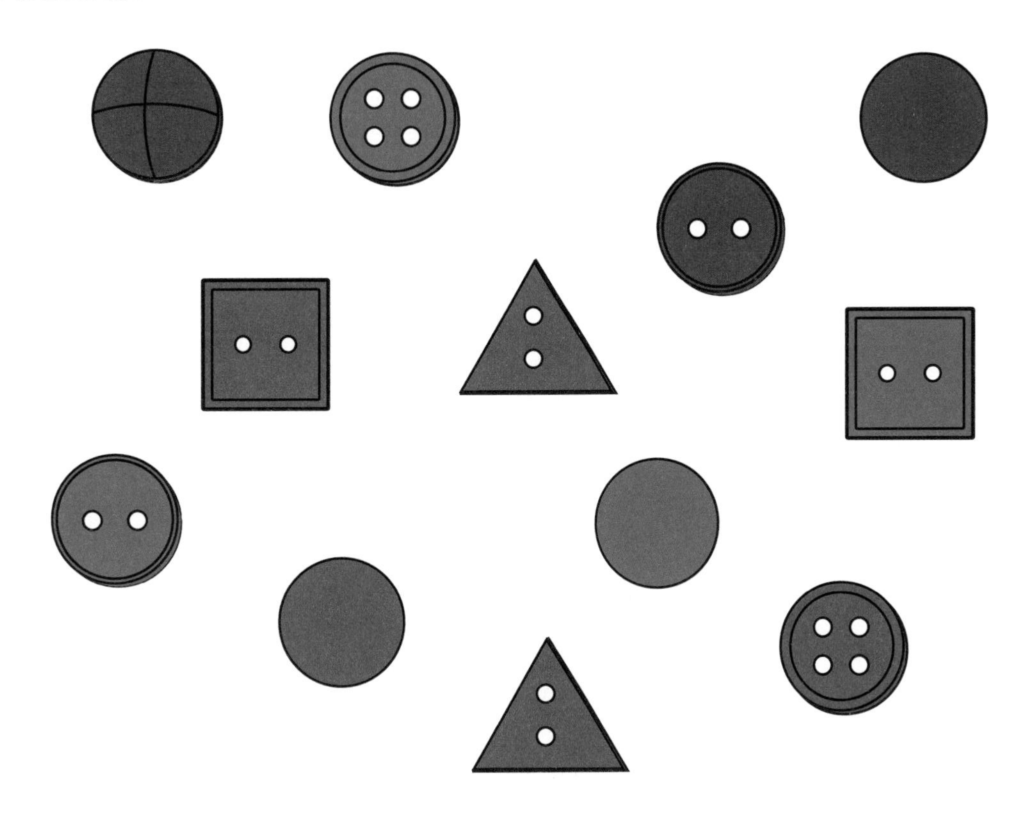

____

____

____

____

____

____

____

Name ______________________ Date ______________

Handful of Buttons 1

Estimate the number of buttons in your handful. Group and count them.

Estimate	Groupings	Count

Name ______________________ Date ______________

Handful of Buttons 2

There were ______________ buttons in my handful.

I grouped them this way:

Class Data Table

Number of Buttons	Number of Children
0 – 9	
10 – 19	
20 – 29	
30 – 39	
40 – 49	
50 – 59	
60 – 69	
70 – 79	
80 – 89	
90 – 99	
	Total:

Name ______________________ Date ______________

Button Sizer

Use the boxes to decide whether your buttons are small, medium, or large.

If a button fits in this box, it is small.

If a button fits in this box but not in the small box, it is medium.

If a button does not fit in the medium box, it is large.

Size	Number of Buttons	Total
Small		
Medium		
Large		

Name ______________________ Date ______________

Button Sizer Graph

Use the information from your data table. Complete the following graph.

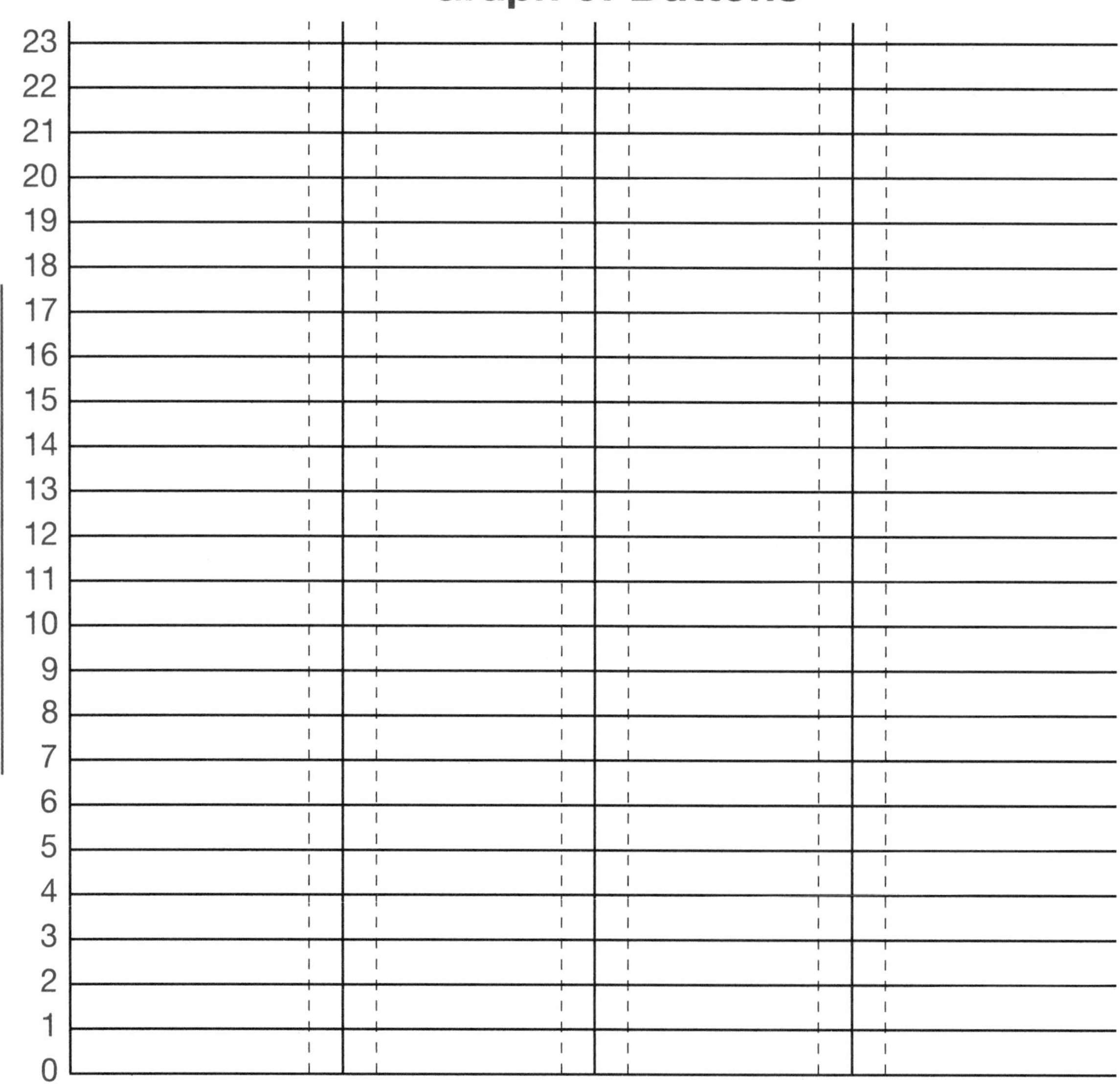

Name ______________________ Date ______________

Triangle Flash Cards: Group A

- **Cut out the flash cards. To practice an addition fact, cover the corner with the highest number. (It is shaded.) Add the two uncovered numbers.**
- **Divide the cards into three piles: those facts you know and can answer quickly, those you can figure out with a strategy, and those you need to learn.**
- **Practice the last two piles again. Then make a list of the facts you need to practice at home.**

Name ______________________ Date ______________

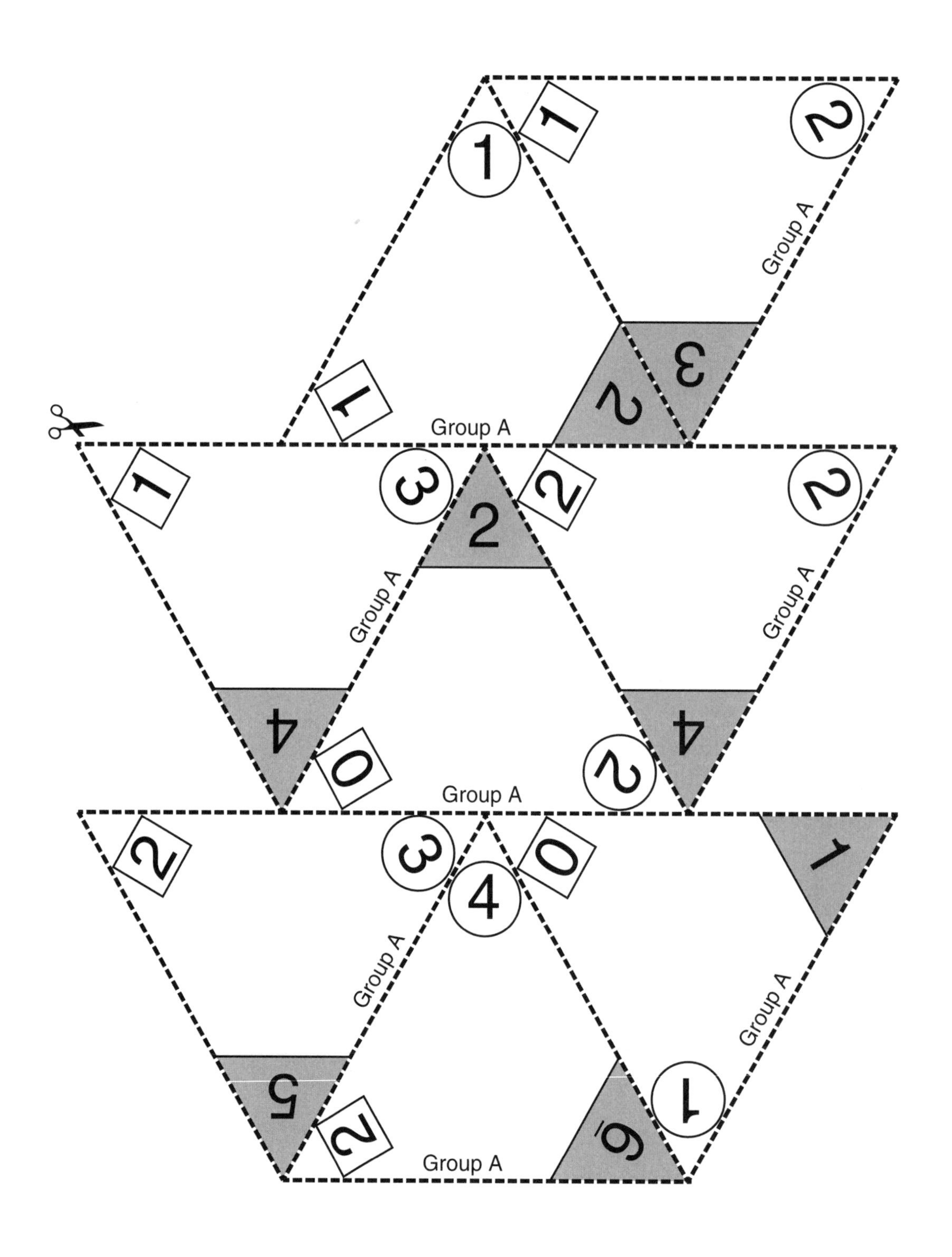

Group A
Group A
Group A
Group A
Group A
Group A
Group A
Group A
Group A

Name ______________________ Date ______________

Triangle Flash Cards: Note Home

Homework

Dear Family Member:

Your child is beginning a systematic study of the addition and subtraction facts. In each unit, your child will study a small group of facts using *Triangle Flash Cards*. In this unit, your child will study the addition facts in Group A (0 + 1, 1 + 1, 2 + 1, 3 + 1, 0 + 2, 2 + 2, 3 + 2, 4 + 2). To help with the study of the facts, follow these directions.

- Choose a card and cover the corner with the largest number. It is shaded. Ask your child to add the two uncovered numbers.

3 + 1 = ?

1 + 3 = ?

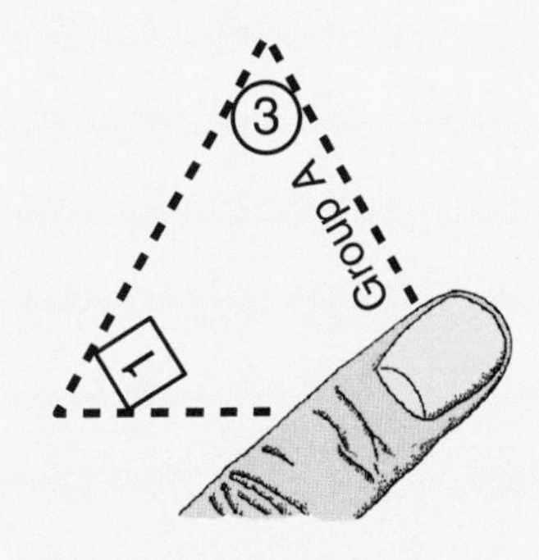

- As you work through the cards, divide them into three piles: those facts your child knows and can answer quickly, those your child can figure out with a strategy, and those your child needs to learn.
- Have your child make a list of the facts in the last two piles for further practice. Concentrate on the facts your child needs to learn.
- Discuss strategies that are useful for learning these facts.
- Practice the last two piles a second time.
- Help your child study these facts for a few minutes each day.

Thank you for your help.

Name ______________________ Date ______________

Button Solutions

Solve each problem. Show how you found the answer.

1. Julia grabbed a handful of buttons. She had 8 red, 6 blue, and 7 orange buttons. How many buttons were in her handful?

2. Sarah had 22 buttons in her collection. She gave 8 to Jeanette and 10 to Eric. How many buttons did she have left?

3. Stephen sorted his buttons into four groups of 5 and 2 buttons left over. How many buttons were in Stephen's handful?

4. Randy sorted his buttons into two groups of 10 and 7 buttons left over. How many buttons did Randy have?

Name ______________________ Date ____________

Bertha's Button Boutique

At Bertha's Button Boutique, you can buy many different types of buttons. The following cards show you four different kinds.

Card A

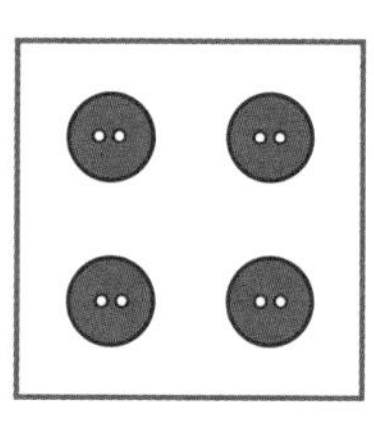

69¢

Card B

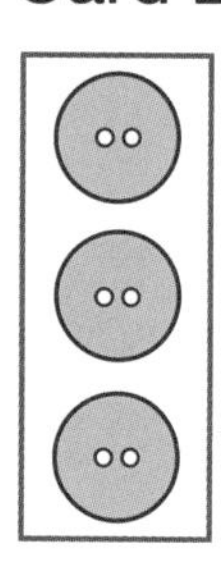

35¢

Card C

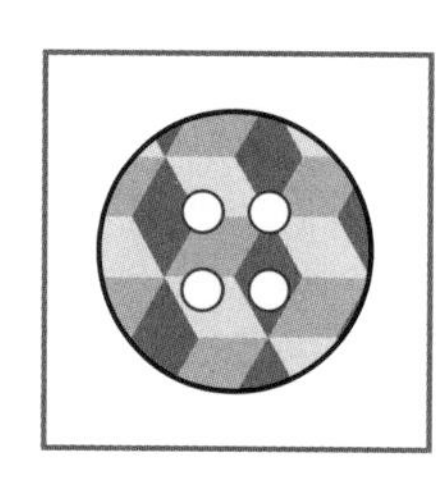

25¢

Card D

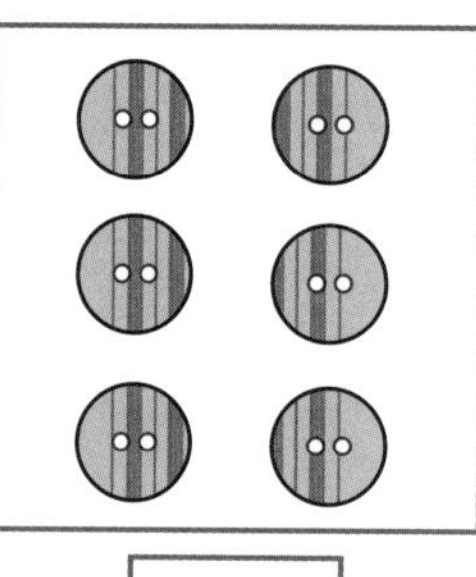

50¢

Solve each problem. Show how you found the answer.

1. Amanda bought Card A and Card B. How much did she spend?

   ____

2. Rachel bought two of Card B. How many buttons did she get?

   ____

   How much did Rachel spend?

   ____

3. Adan likes the buttons on Card D. If he buys two of Card D, how many buttons will he get?

   ____

4. Thomas bought Card C and Card D. How much did he spend?

   ____

Name ______________________________ Date ________________

Button Place Value Tables

My group counted these buttons:

Hundreds	Tens	Ones

My group counted ________ buttons.

Our class counted these buttons:

Hundreds	Tens	Ones

Our class has a total of ________ buttons.

Name ______________________________ Date ________________

Guess and Group

Homework

Dear Family Member:

In class, your child grabbed a handful of buttons, grouped them into piles of ten, and recorded the number of tens and buttons left over. Give your child a bowl filled with objects such as pennies, popcorn, cereal, or beads to use for the work on this page.

Thank you for your cooperation.

Take two handfuls from the bowl.

What objects did you grab? ________________

Estimate: I grabbed about ________________ objects.

Tens	Ones

Group the objects into piles of ten. How many groups of ten do you have? How many ones are left over? Record your answers in the first row in the table.

Write a sentence describing your handfuls. Include the type of object and how many you grabbed.

____

Ask a family member to take two handfuls. Estimate the number he or she pulled. Group the objects. Complete the second row in the table. Then record the actual number.

Estimate ________________ Actual Number ________________

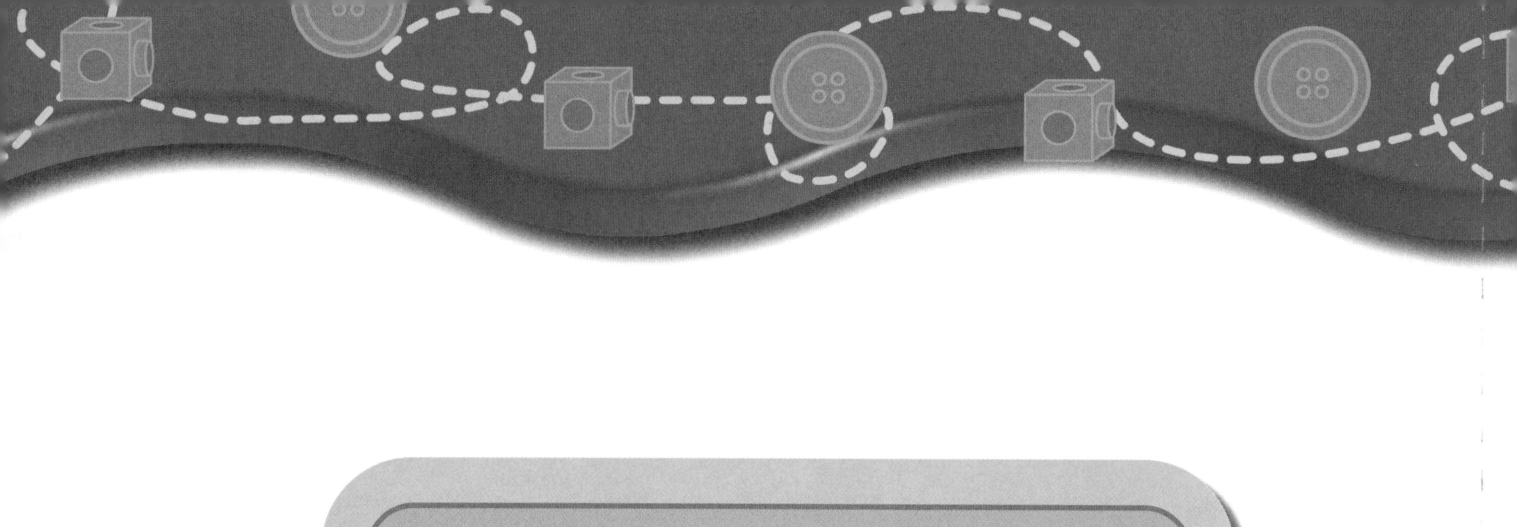

Unit 4

Working with Data

	Student Guide	Adventure Book	Unit Resource Guide*
Lesson 1			
High, Wide, and Handsome	●		
Lesson 2			
Are They Related?	●		
Lesson 3			
How Do They Compare?	●		●
Lesson 4			
When Close Is Good Enough	●		

***Unit Resource Guide* pages are from the teacher materials.**

Name ______________________ Date ______________

High, Wide, and Handsome

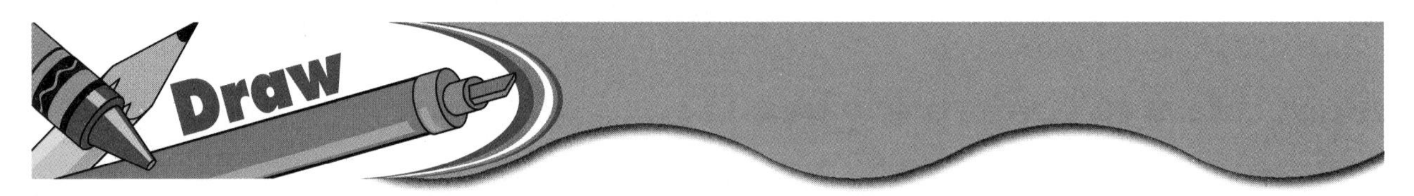

Draw a picture of the lab. Be sure to show height (*H*) and arm span (*AS*).

Name ______________________ Date ______________

Measure the height and arm span for each student in your group.

Name	*H* Height (in ______ *unit*)	*AS* Arm Span (in ______ *unit*)

1. What is the shortest arm span in your group?

____

2. What is the tallest height in your group?

____

3. What is the difference between the tallest height and the shortest height?

____

Name ______________________ Date ______________

Arm Span Graph

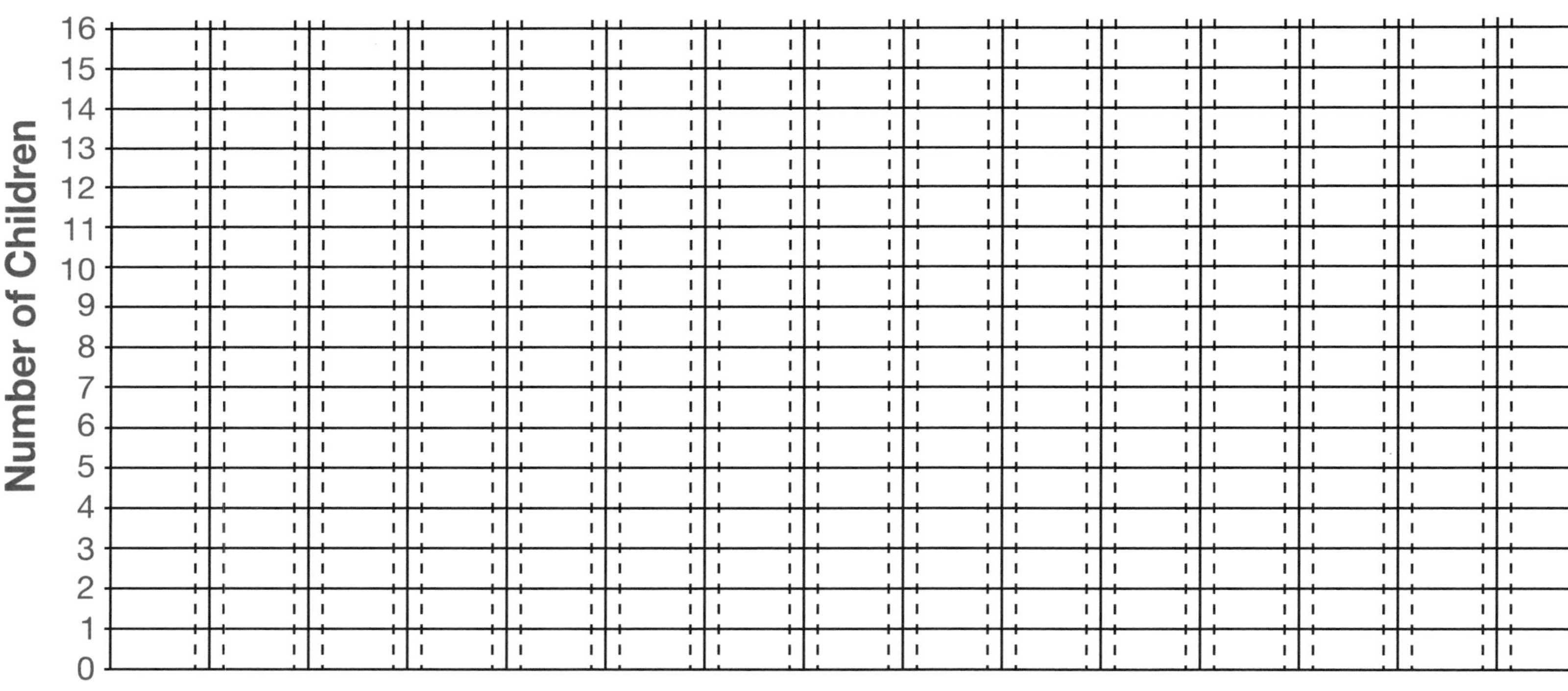

Name ______________________ Date ______________

Graph

Height Graph

Number of Children
C

16
15
14
13
12
11
10
9
8
7
6
5
4
3
2
1
0

Height (in links)
H

Name ______________________ Date ______________

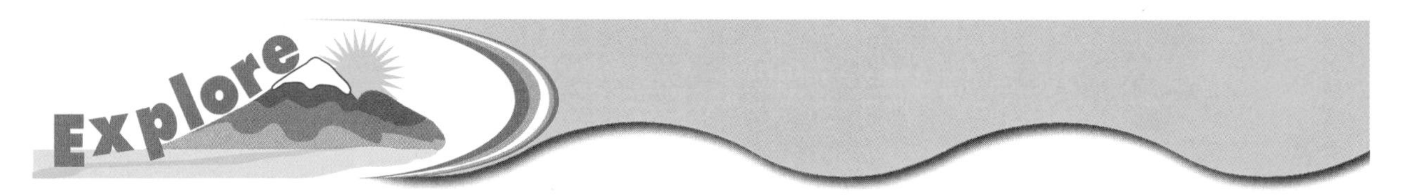

Answer the following questions using the class data table.

4. Look at the tallest height and the shortest height. What is the range for height?

____

5. Look at the longest arm span and the shortest arm span. What is the range for arm span?

____

6. Maria's arm span is 33 links. How many links tall is Maria? Explain your thinking.

____

____

7. Imagine you have identical twins in your class. Would you expect their arm spans to be the same? Would you expect their heights to be the same? Explain your thinking.

____

____

Name ______________________ Date ______________

Colors of Shoes at My House

Dear Family Member:

Over the next few days, your child will collect and analyze data about the shoes in your home. As the assignment progresses, please help your child illustrate his or her data gathering, fill in the data table, make a graph, and answer the questions.

Thank you for your help.

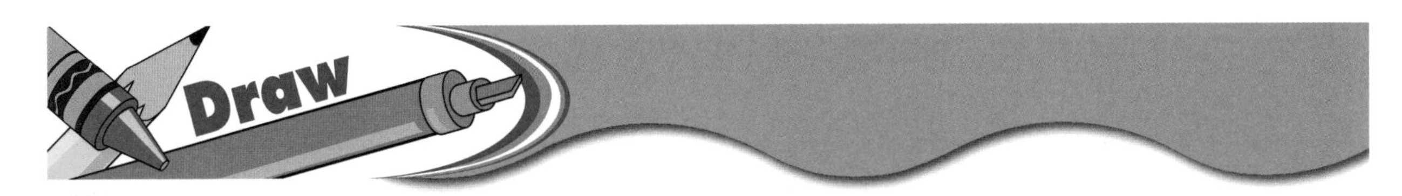

Choose three colors of shoes. Find the number of pairs of shoes of each color. Draw a picture that shows what you will do.

Name ______________________ Date ______________

Fill in the table with data collected at home. Then graph the data.

C Colors of Shoes	*P* Number of Pairs

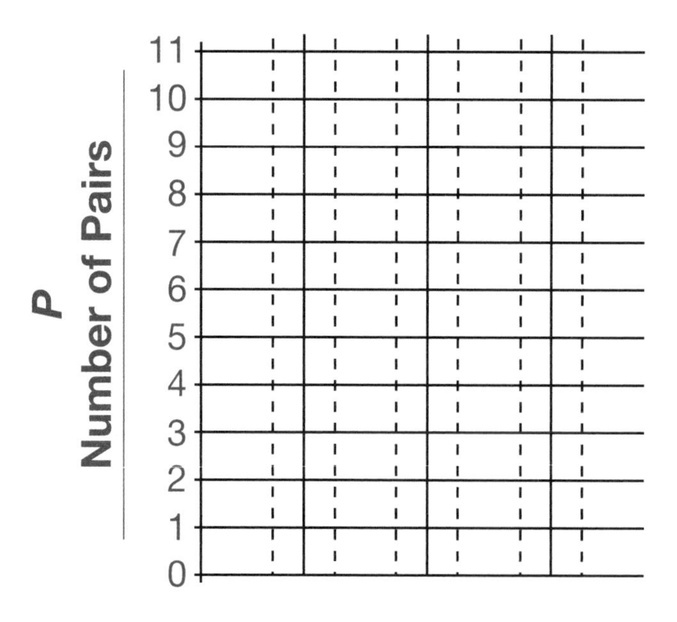

Name ______________________ Date ______________

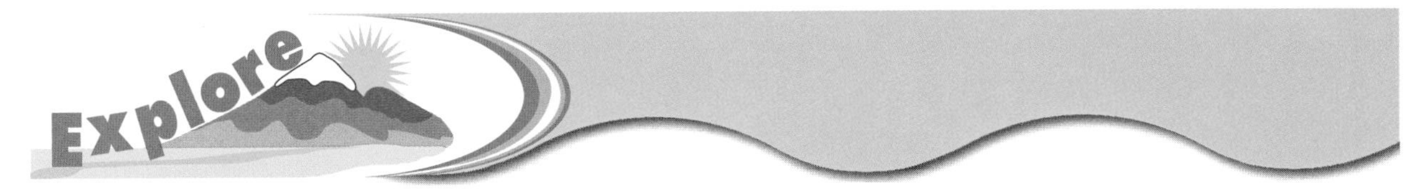

Answer the following questions based on your data table.

1. Which is the most common shoe color?

   ____

2. Which is the least common shoe color?

   ____

3. How many pairs of shoes are there?

   ____

4. How many shoes are there altogether?

   ____

5. What is the range for the number of pairs of shoes?

   ____

Name ______________________ Date ______________

Triangle Flash Cards: Group B

- Cut out the flash cards. To practice an addition fact, cover the corner with the highest number. (It is shaded.) Add the two uncovered numbers.
- Divide the cards into three piles: those facts you know and can answer quickly, those you can figure out with a strategy, and those you need to learn.
- Practice the last two piles again. Then make a list of the facts you need to practice at home.

Name ______________________ Date ____________

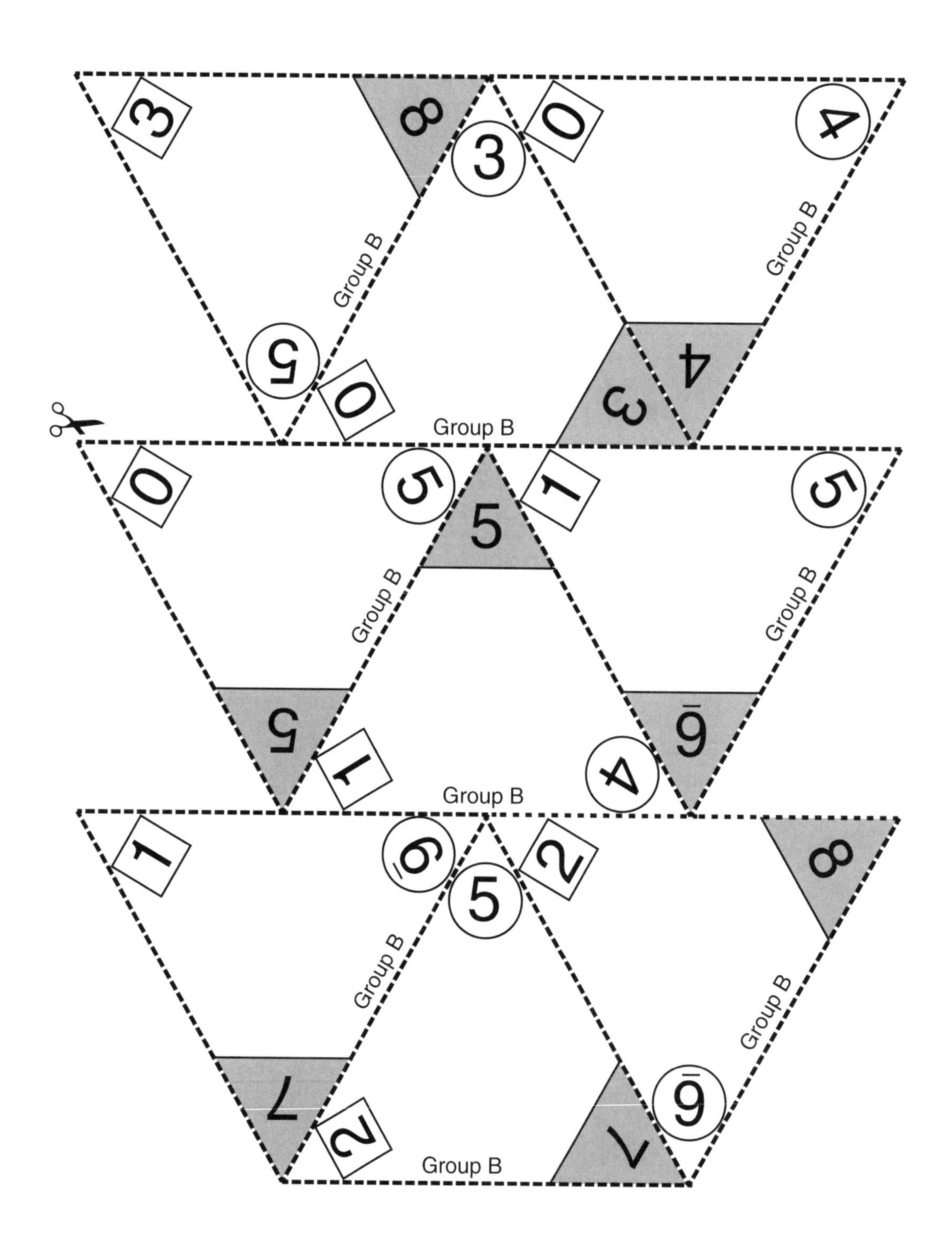

3
8
3
0
4
Group B
Group B
5
0
4
3
Group B
0
5
5
1
5
Group B
Group B
5
1
4
6
Group B
1
6
5
2
8
Group B
Group B
7
2
7
6
Group B

Name ______________________ Date ______________

Three Rectangles

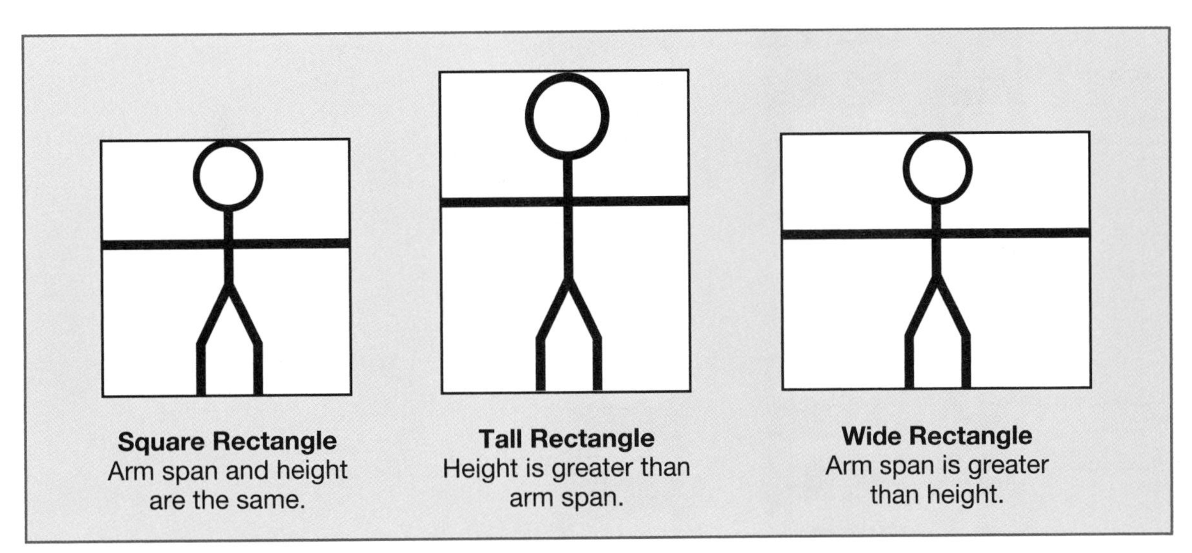

Complete the following sentences.

I am __________ links tall.

My arm span is __________ links.

The difference between my height and arm span is __________.

My height and arm span make a __________ rectangle shape.

Name ______________________ Date ______________

Height and Arm Span Graph

Number the vertical axis. Then graph the data.

L
Number of Links

Height
H

Arm Span
AS

Name ______________________ Date ______________

Type of Rectangle

Write the total of the tallies in the third column.

Miss Ozima's Class Rectangles

Type of Rectangle	Tallies	Total
Square Rectangle Arm span and height are the same.	卌 卌 |||	
Tall Rectangle Height is greater than arm span.	卌 卌 ||||	
Wide Rectangle Arm span is greater than height.	||	

Name ______________________ Date ______________

Use the information from Miss Ozima's class. Make a bar graph. Number the vertical axis by ones.

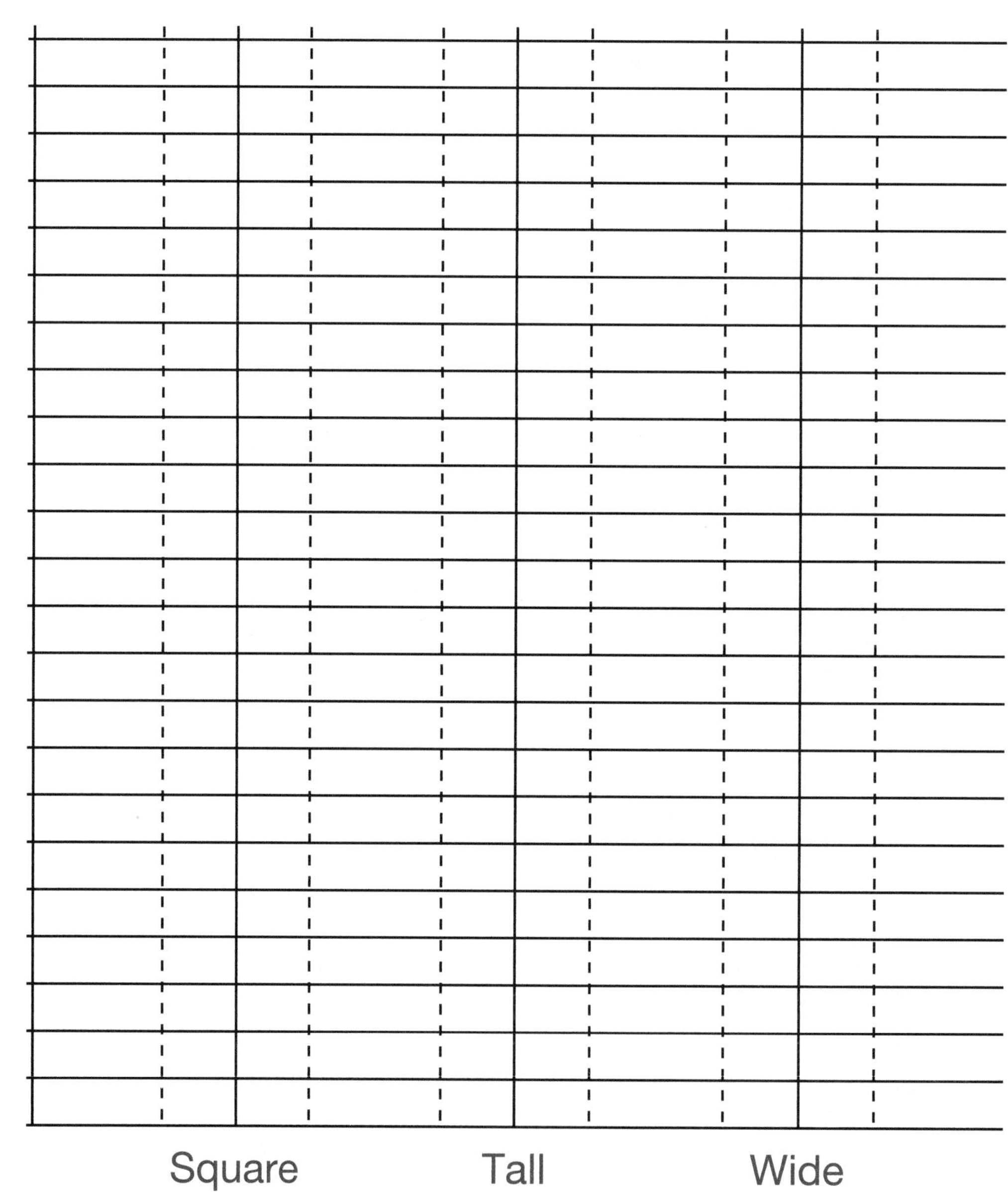

Name ______________________ Date ____________

Making Comparisons

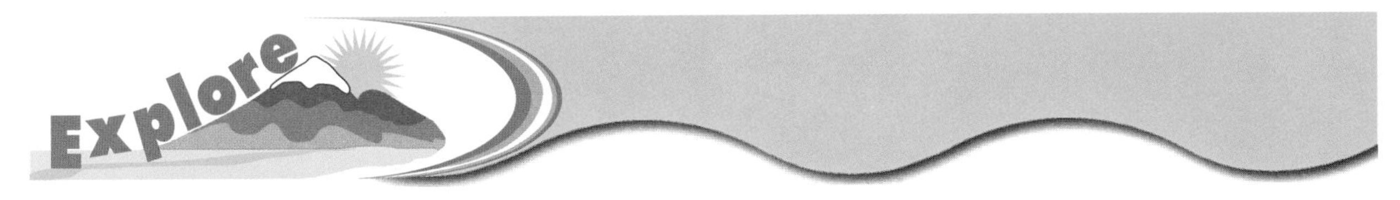

Compare your class data with data from another class. Use the graphs to answer the questions below.

How are the two data collections alike? How are they different? Make lists to show your findings.

Alike:

____

____

____

____

____

Different:

____

____

____

____

____

Name ______________________________ Date ____________________

Hand Spans and Cubits

Measure each of the items below. First use your hand span to measure the items. Then use your cubit. Measure two more objects or distances of your choice. Add them to the data table.

Object or Distance	Hand Spans	Cubits	
width of desk			
teacher's desk to door			
height of chalk rail			
teacher's desk to sharpener			
height of filing cabinet			

Choose a third measurement tool. Label the fourth column. Measure the objects and distances using this tool.

Name ______________________ Date ____________

My Desk: Guess and Check

1. I estimate that the height of my desk is about

   ________ hand spans.

2. Measure the height of your desk using hand spans. My desk is about

   ________ hand spans.

3. What do you think about when you make an estimate?

   ____

   ____

   ____

4. I estimate that the height of my desk is about ________ cubits.

5. Measure the height of your desk using cubits. My desk is

   about ________ cubits.

6. Choose something else to measure in the room.

   My ________ is about ________ hand spans.

   My ________ is about ________ cubits.

Name ______________________ Date ______________

Handy Measurements at Home

Dear Family Member:

Your child is learning to measure using his or her hand span and cubit. These units of measure are illustrated in the picture. Please help your child select some objects to measure and complete the assignment.

Thank you.

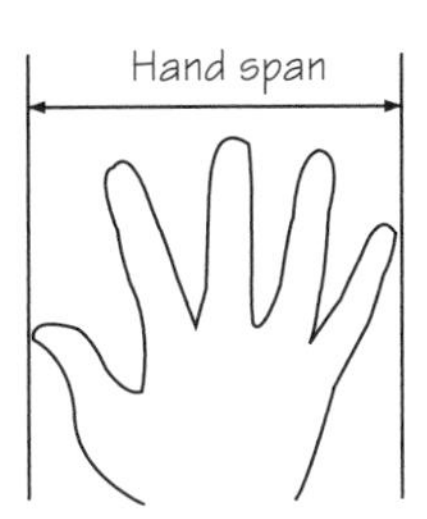

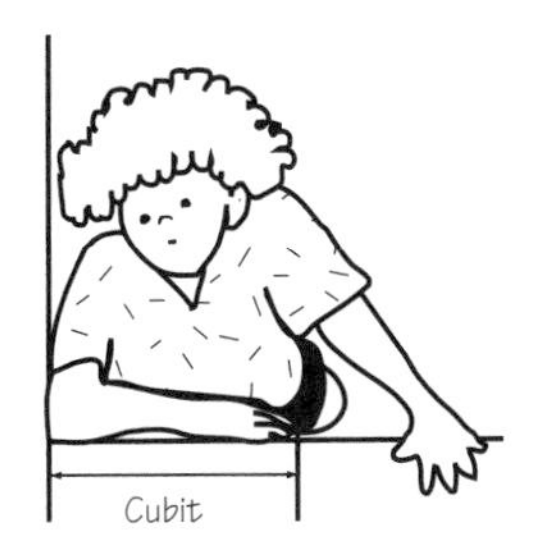

Measure three objects or distances with your hand span and cubit. Predict what a family member's measurements will be. Record his or her measurements and check your predictions.

Object or Distance	My Hand Spans	Prediction	Your Hand Spans
width of refrigerator			

Object or Distance	My Cubits	Prediction	Your Cubits
width of refrigerator			

Name ______________________ Date ______________

Could Be or Crazy?

Circle whether each statement "could be" true or whether it is "crazy."

1. Tasha measured her dog's tail. It was 2 hand spans long.

   Could Be Crazy

2. Fred is a second grader. He measured his height in cubits. He measured 30 cubits tall.

   Could Be Crazy

3. Linda says her kitchen table is 4 cubits long. She says it is 4 hand spans long too.

   Could Be Crazy

4. Connie said, "My hair is about 1 cubit long."

   Could Be Crazy

5. Mark's dad says the width of the doorway is 5 hand spans. Mark, a second grader, measured 3 hand spans.

   Could Be Crazy

6. Choose one of the statements. Explain how you decided whether it was a "could be" or a "crazy" statement.

   ____

   ____

   ____

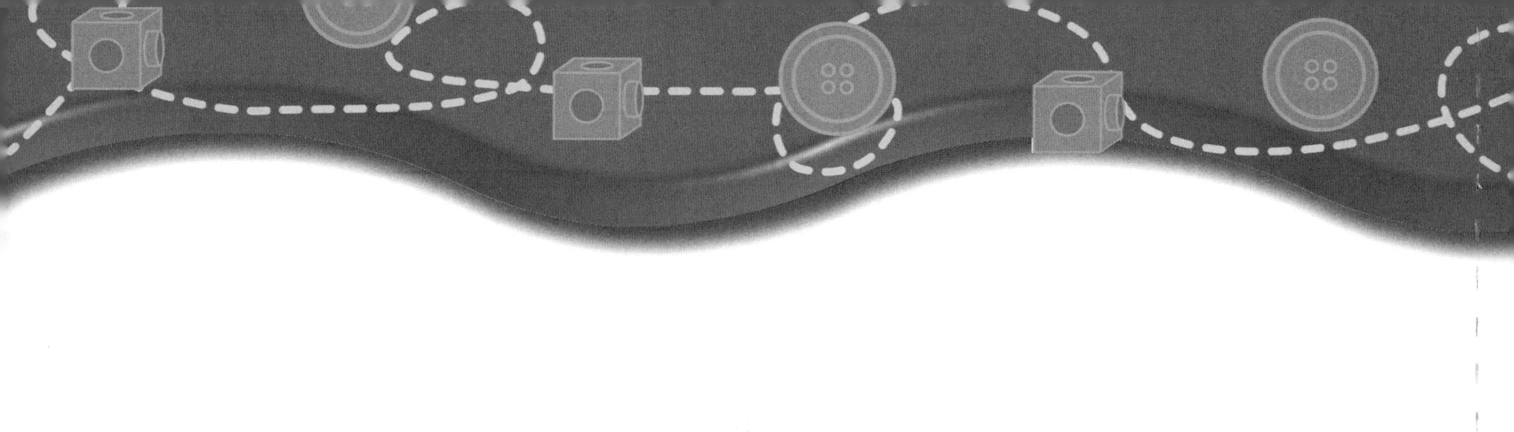

Unit 5

Going to Great Lengths

	Student Guide	Adventure Book	Unit Resource Guide*
Lesson 1			
The Long and Short of It	●		
Lesson 2			
Exploring the Number Line	●		
Lesson 3			
Centimeters and Meters	●		
Lesson 4			
Rolling Along in Centimeters	●		
Lesson 5			
Mine Is the Best: The Challenge		●	

******Unit Resource Guide* **pages are from the teacher materials.**

Name ______________________________ Date ________________

Measurement Interval

Predict three objects that fit in each interval. Then use a chain of links to measure each length.

0–50 Links

Object	Length (in links)

51–100 Links

Object	Length (in links)

101–150 Links

Object	Length (in links)

Name ______________________ Date ______________

Triangle Flash Cards: Group C

- Cut out the flash cards. To practice an addition fact, cover the corner with the highest number. (It is shaded.) Add the two uncovered numbers.
- Divide the cards into three piles: those facts you know and can answer quickly, those you can figure out with a strategy, and those you need to learn.
- Practice the last two piles again.

Name ________________________ Date ______________

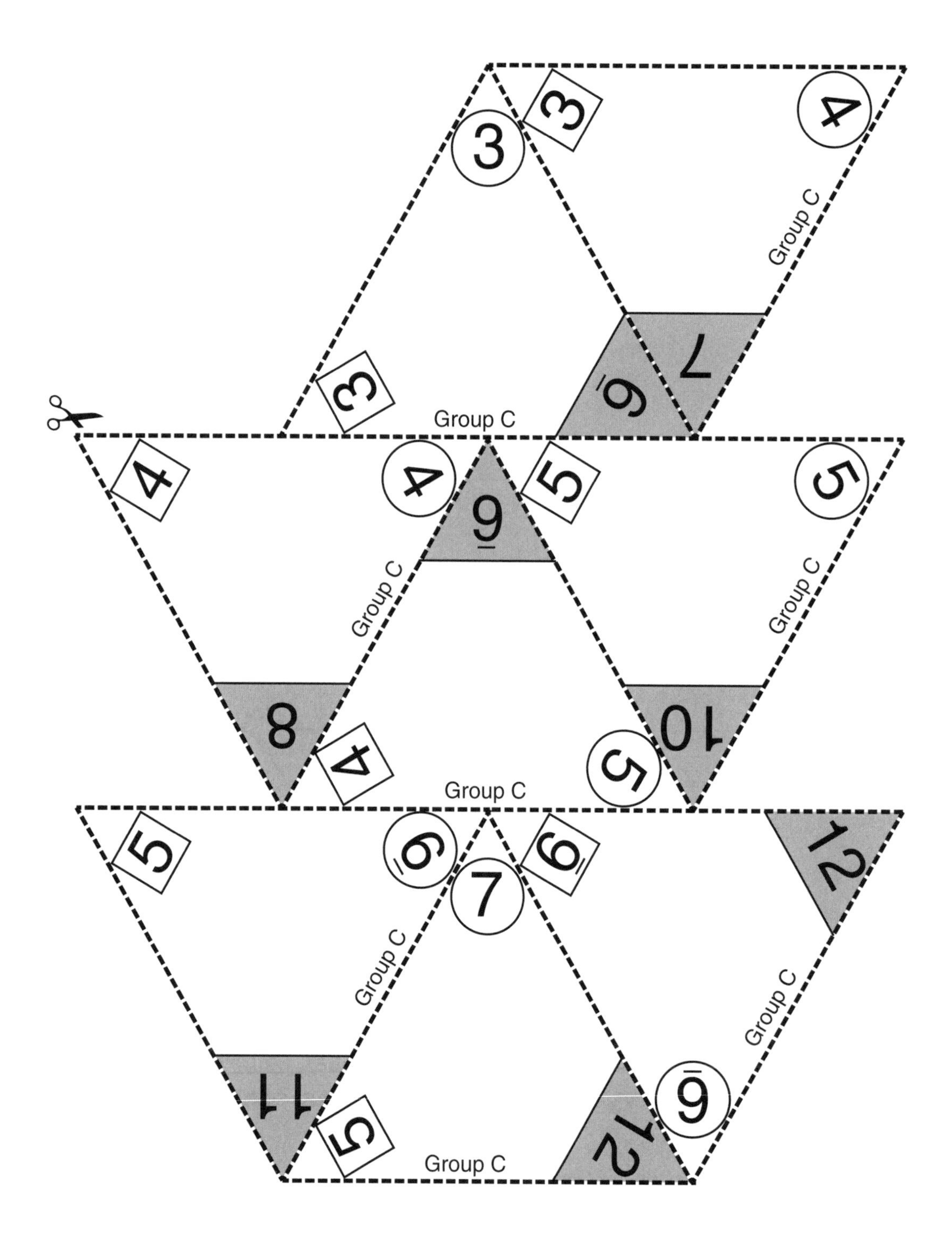

3
3
4
Group C
7
9
3
Group C
4
4
9
5
5
Group C
Group C
8
4
10
5
Group C
5
9
7
9
12
Group C
Group C
11
5
12
9
Group C

Name ______________________ Date ______________

What's My Location?

Fill in the missing numbers on each number line.

A.

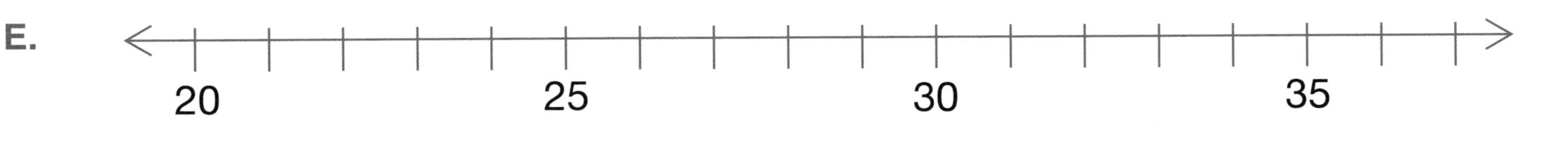

B.

C.

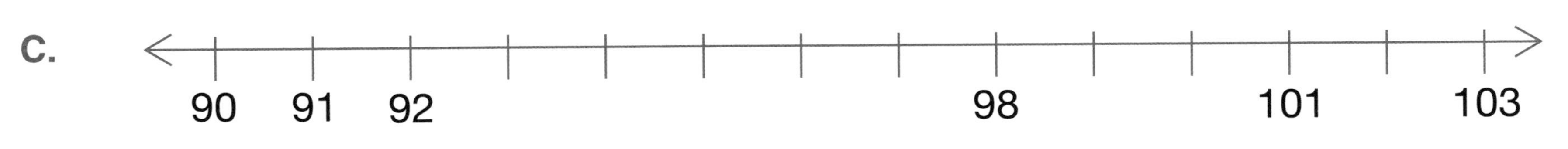

D.

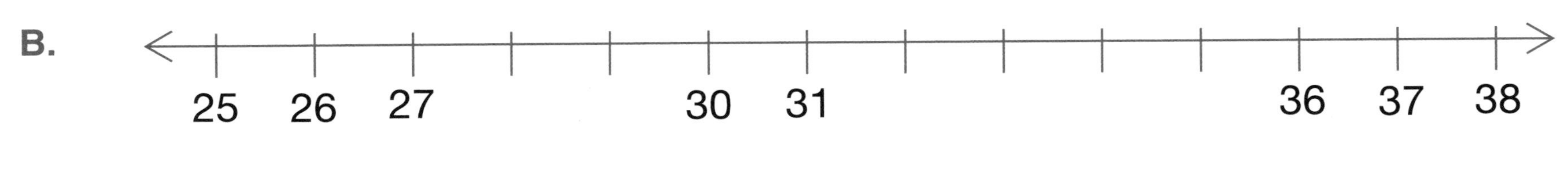

E.

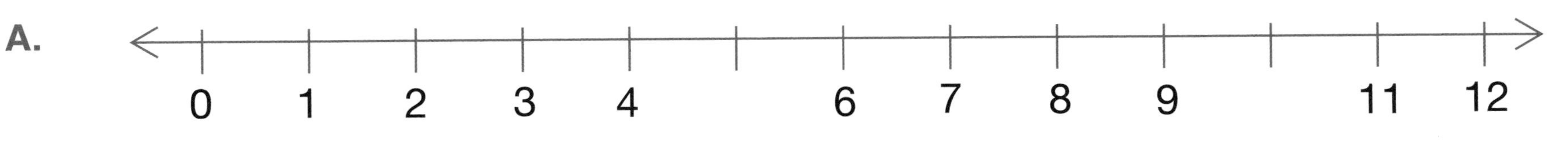

Name ______________________________ Date ________________

Number Lines

As your teacher calls out numbers, write them on the number line.

A.

B.

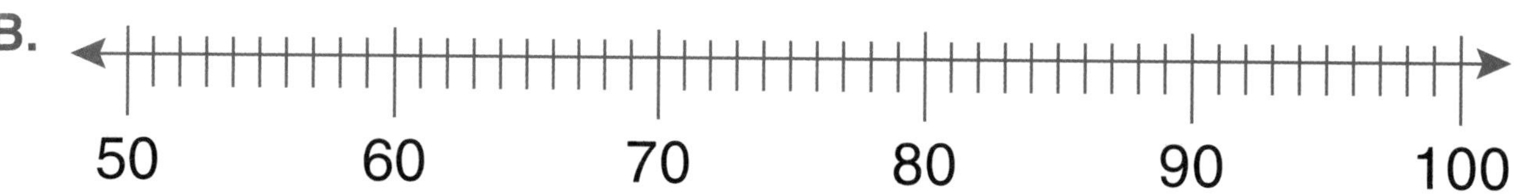

C.

D.

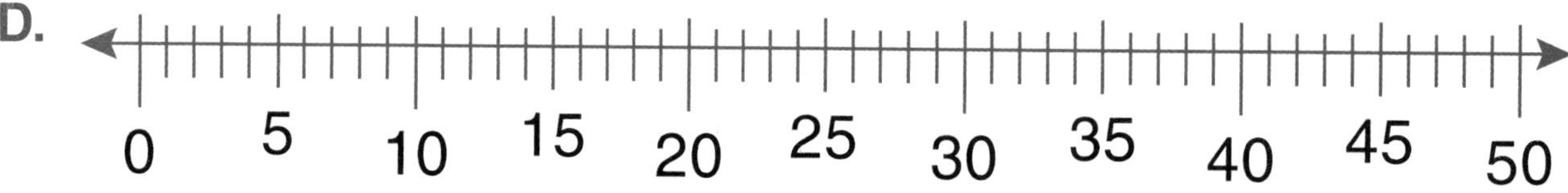

E.

Name ______________________ Date ____________

Number Line for Heights

Dear Family Member:

This number line shows the numbers 1 to 80. Your child is learning to place numbers on the correct point on the line. Help your child find the height in inches of each family member and place the height in the correct place on the line.

Thank you for your cooperation.

Find the height in inches of each of your family members. Record the numbers on the number line.

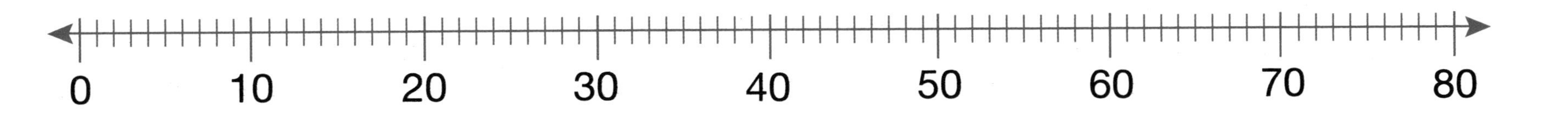

Name ______________________ Date ____________

My Own Number Line

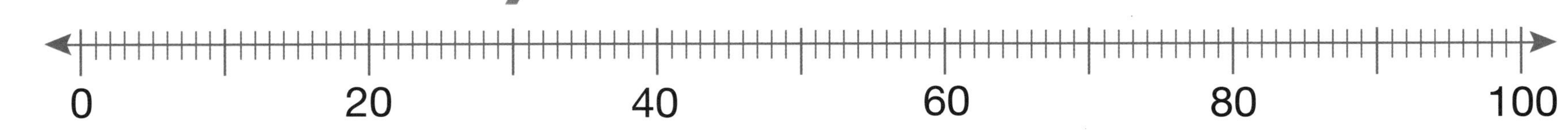

My number is ________. Place the number on the number line.

I know it goes where I put it because ______________________

Name ______________________ Date ______________

Building a Meter Tape

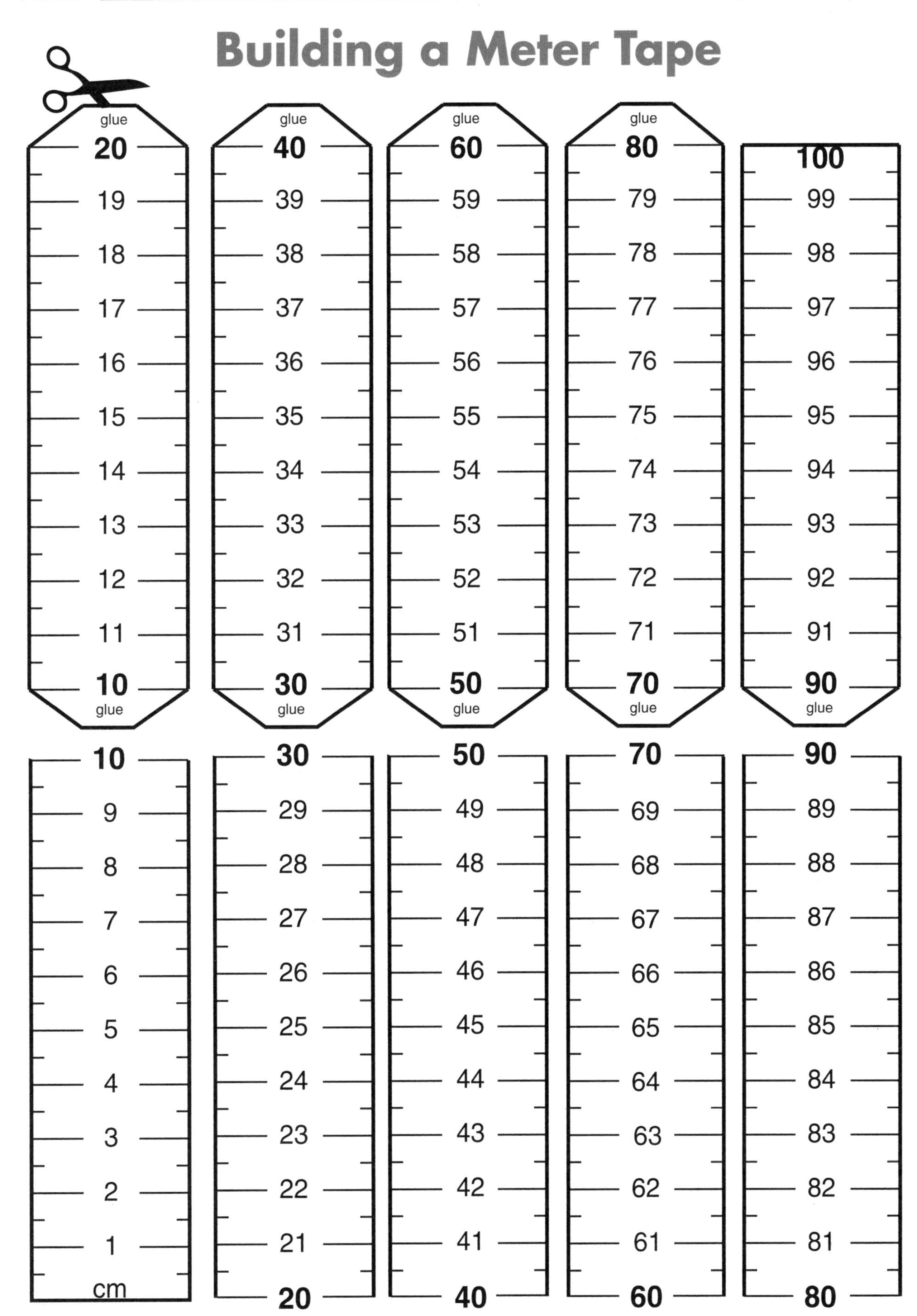

Name ______________________ Date ______________

Measuring Small Objects

Use your meter tape or a meterstick.

1. How wide is your index finger? ________ cm

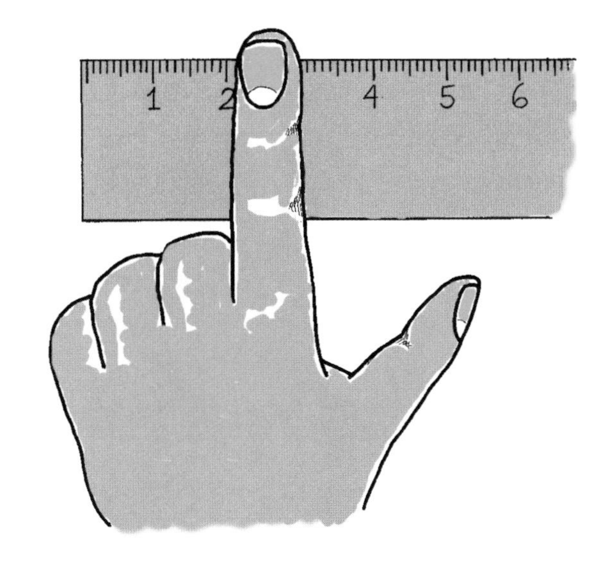

2. How long is the pencil? ________ cm

3. How long is this paper? ________ cm

4. Your choice: ______________________ ________ cm
item name

Name ______________________ Date ______________

Measuring Big Objects

Use your paper meter tape or a meterstick.

1. How high is your desk?

_________ cm

2. How tall are you? Have a classmate help measure your height.

_________ cm

3. Are you exactly one meter tall?

____

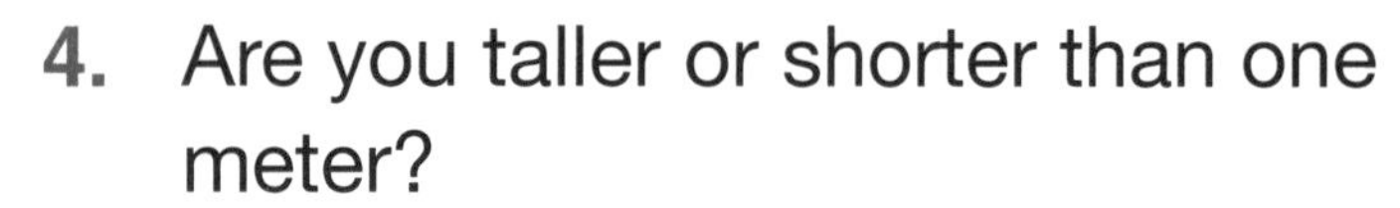

4. Are you taller or shorter than one meter?

____

5. How high is it from the windowsill to the floor?

_________ cm

Is this exactly one meter? _________

Is this more or less than one meter?

____

Name ______________________ Date ______________

Estimating and Measuring

Find objects in the room. Estimate their lengths. Then measure them.

Centimeters

Object	Estimation (centimeters)	Measurement (centimeters)
Eraser	5 cm	3 cm

Meters and Centimeters

Object	Estimation (m and cm)	Measurement (m and cm)

Name ______________________ Date ______________

10-centimeter Treasure Hunt

Dear Family Member:

Your child is learning to estimate and measure length. Help your child complete the problems below.

Thank you for your help.

Use your paper meter tape. Look for objects that measure close to 10 centimeters. List the name of each object you find.

1. ______________________

2. ______________________

3. ______________________

4. ______________________

5. ______________________

Challenge:

Find objects or distances that measure close to 1 meter. List the name of each object or distance you find.

1. ______________________

2. ______________________

Name ______________________ Date ______________

Tony at the Ballpark

Tony wrote the following story about measurements.

"My uncle took me to a baseball game. The White Sox played the Yankees. The ballpark was so big! We walked 80 **centimeters** to get to our seats. I bought a large soda about 1 **meter** tall and a hot dog 20 **centimeters** long. The food was great! A White Sox player hit a home run. The ball must have gone 100 **centimeters!** A fan with a baseball glove 1 **meter** wide caught the ball. It was a wonderful day."

Complete the table using Tony's measurements. Which ones "could be" correct measurements, and which are "crazy"?

Object or Distance	Measurement	Could Be or Crazy
walk to seats		
large soda		
hot dog		
home run		
baseball glove		

Change Tony's story so it makes sense.

Name ____________________ Date ____________

Rolling Along in Centimeters

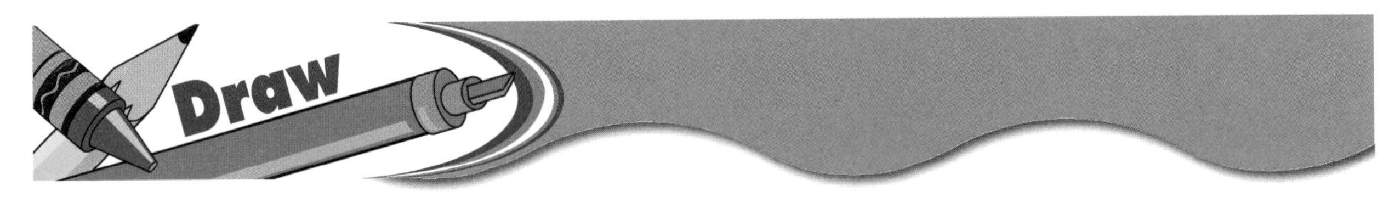

Draw a picture to show how you will set up the lab. Be sure to show the two main variables.

What two main variables are we studying in this lab?

____

What should stay the same each time the car is rolled?

____

____

Name ______________________________ Date ____________________

Work with your group to test each car. Record your data in the table below.

T Type of Car	*D* Distance in ____________ unit			
	Trial 1	Trial 2	Trial 3	Median
Sample				

Name ______________________ Date ______________

Make a bar graph of your data.

Name ______________________________ Date ______________

Explore

1. A. Which car rolled the longest distance?

____

D = ______________________________

B. Which car rolled the shortest distance?

____

D = ______________________________

C. What is the difference between the longest and the shortest distances? Show how you found your answer.

____

2. You want to see which car is the best roller in the class. Can you tell using only your group's data table? Why or why not?

____

____

3. The teacher asked Debbie how far her car rolled. "It rolled 132," Debbie said. What is wrong with Debbie's answer?

____

Name ______________________ Date ______________

Franco's Data

Franco's team found the data shown in the graph below.

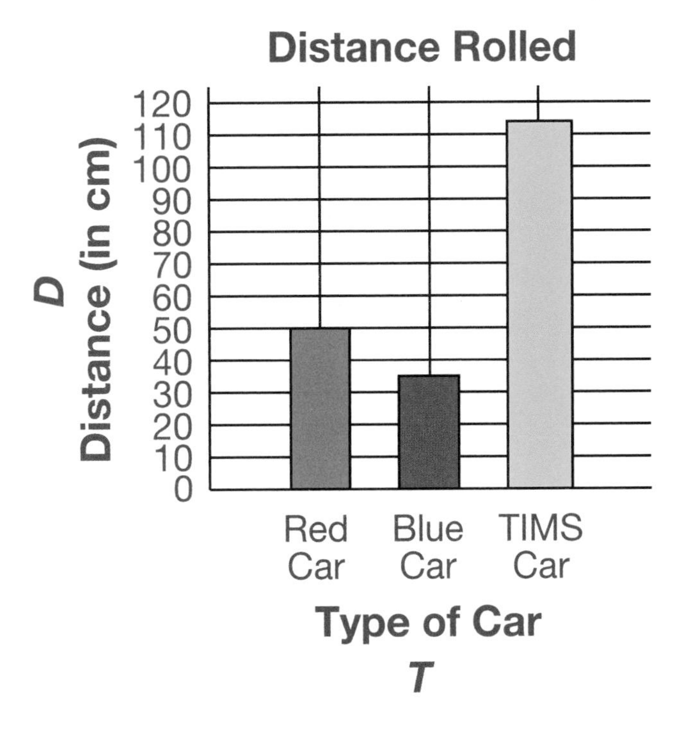

1. How far did the TIMS car roll?

____

2. How much farther did the TIMS car roll than the Red Car? Tell how you know.

____

____

3. Name at least one other thing you know by reading this graph.

____

____

Name ________________________ Date ________________

Thumbs Up

Dear Family Member:

Your child is learning to measure with a meter tape. The thumb measurement should be taken from the tip to the base of the thumb (the second knuckle). Assist your child in measuring each of his or her fingers as well as those of a family member. Use the paper meter tape your child made in school or a ruler that indicates centimeters.

Thank you.

Measure the thumbs of family members. Write the measurements in the table.

Family Member	Thumb Length (in centimeters)

Name ______________________ Date ______________

My Finger Measurements

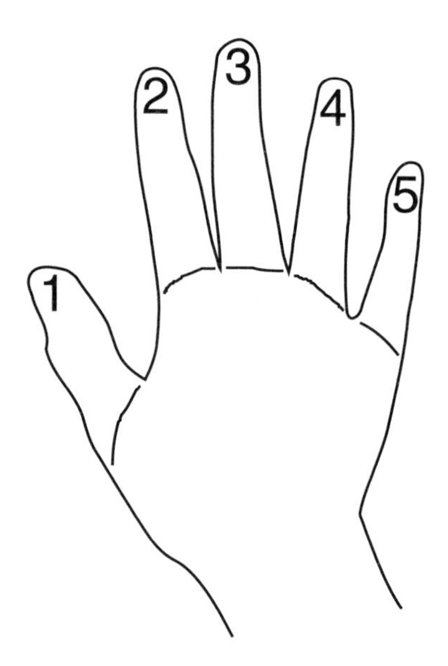

1. Thumb ______________ cm
2. Index ______________ cm
3. Middle ______________ cm
4. Ring ______________ cm
5. Little ______________ cm

Choose a family member. Do you think his or her fingers will be the same, longer, or shorter than your fingers?

____

Measure and find out.

My ______________'s Finger Measurements

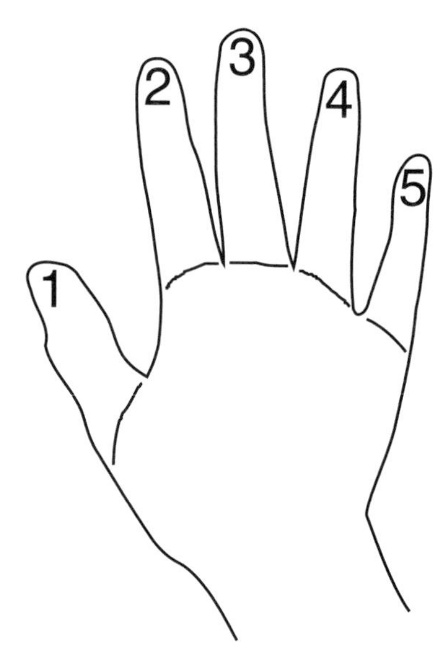

1. Thumb ______________ cm
2. Index ______________ cm
3. Middle ______________ cm
4. Ring ______________ cm
5. Little ______________ cm

Name ______________________ Date ______________

Rolling Cars: Partner Problems

Two cars rolling down the ramps are shown below. In this drawing, we are looking down from above.

Ramp

A

cm 10 20 30 40 50 60 70 80 90 100 cm 10 20 30 40 50 60 70 80

1st Meterstick

2nd Meterstick

Ramp

B

1. How far did Car A roll? ______________________

2. How far did Car B roll? ______________________

3. How much farther did Car B roll than Car A? Show how you found your answer.

____

____

4. Did Car B roll twice as far as Car A? How do you know?

____

____

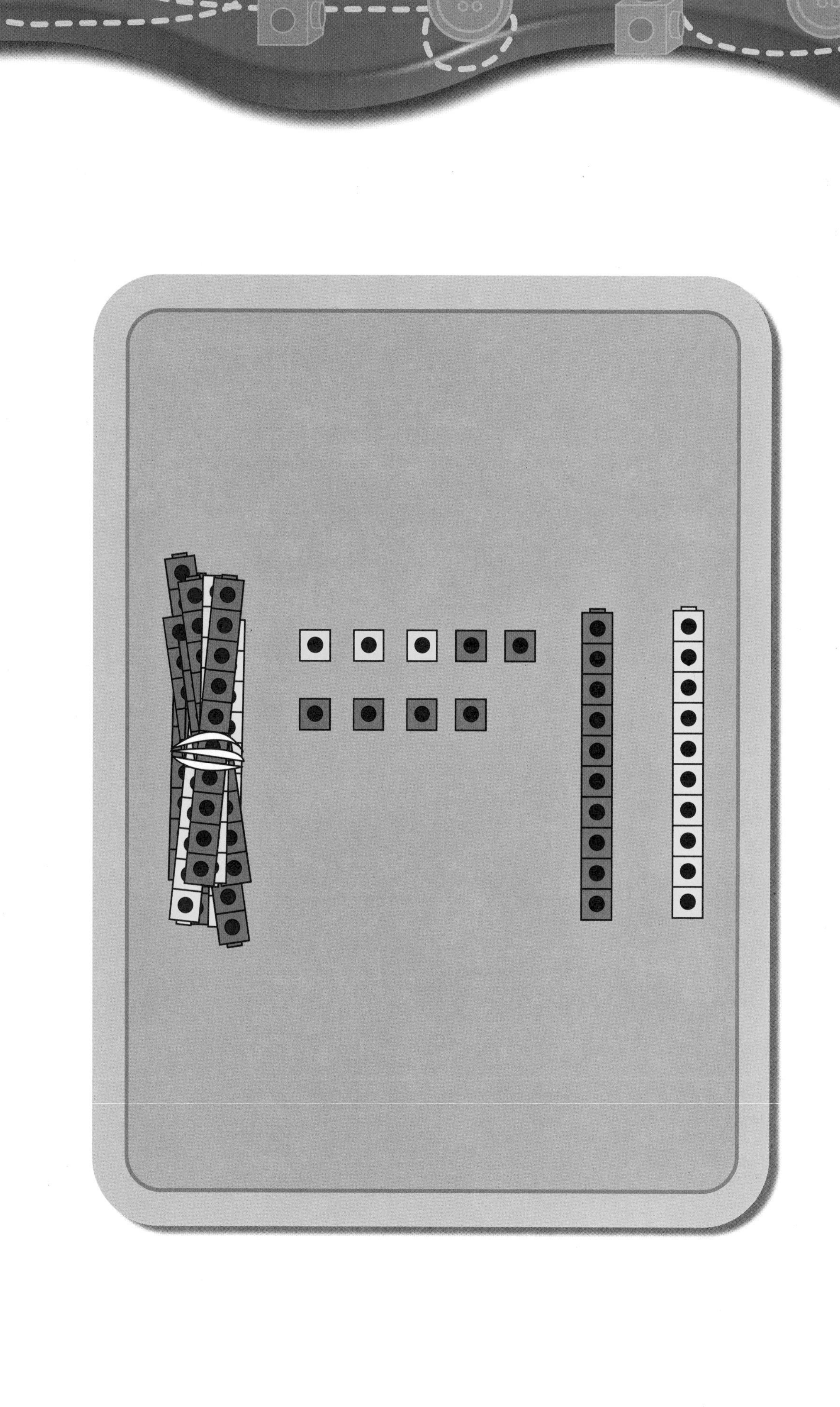

Unit 6

Putting Numbers in Their Places

	Student Guide	Adventure Book	Unit Resource Guide*
Lesson 1			
Take Your Time	●		
Lesson 2			
Pasta Place Value	●		
Lesson 3			
Every Number Has Its Place	●		●
Lesson 4			
Take Your Places, Please	●		
Lesson 5			
Marshmallows and Containers	●		
Lesson 6			
The Princess and Her Playmate		●	

***Unit Resource Guide* pages are from the teacher materials.**

Name ____________________ Date ____________________

Make Your Own

Cut out the clocks and hands below.

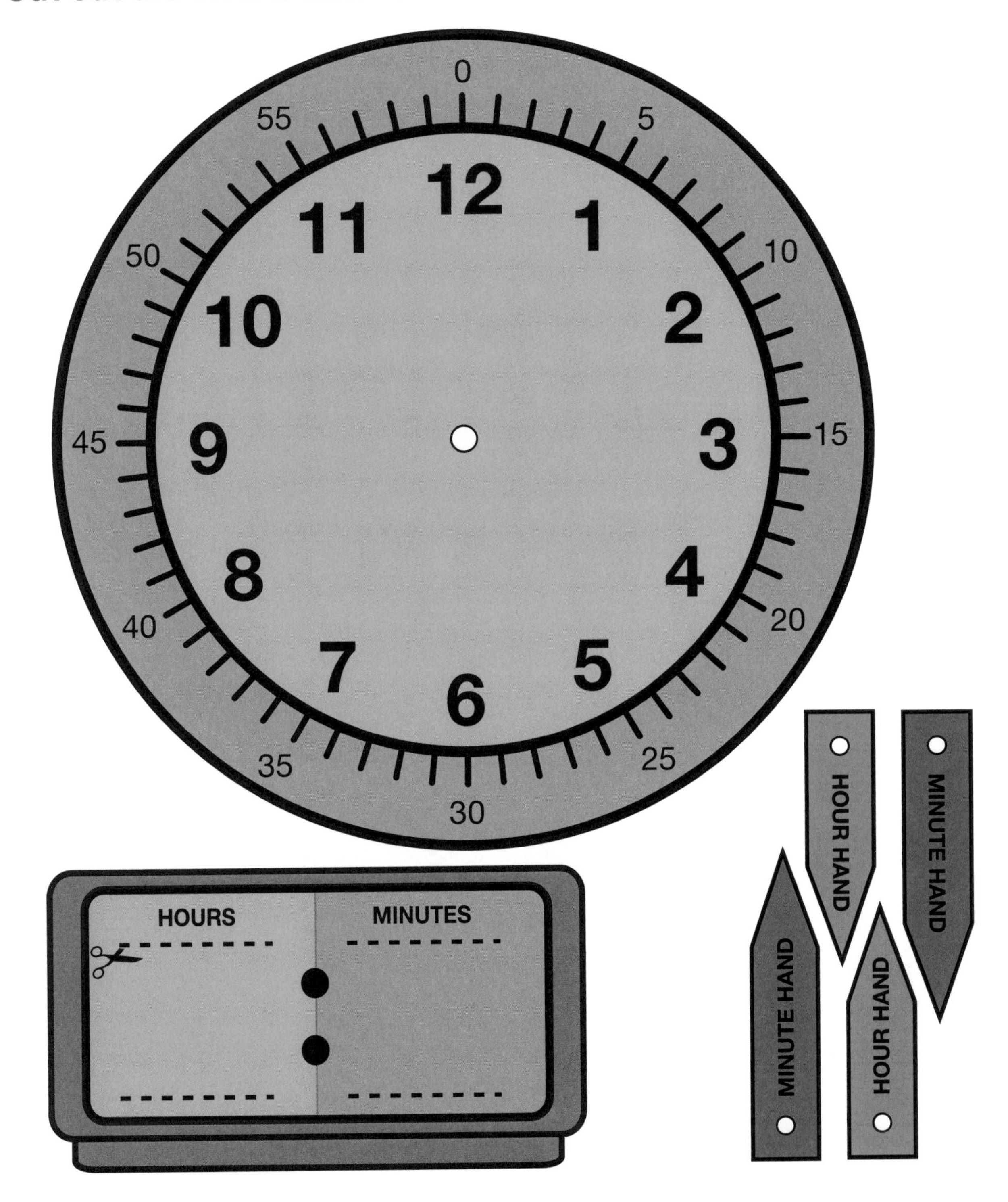

Name ______________________ Date ______________

Cut out each strip. Cut only on the dotted lines.

HOURS		MINUTES	
1	7	00	30
2	8	05	35
3	9	10	40
4	10	15	45
5	11	20	50
6	12	25	55

Name ______________________ Date ______________

Clocks

Write the times on the clocks below.

1.

______

2.

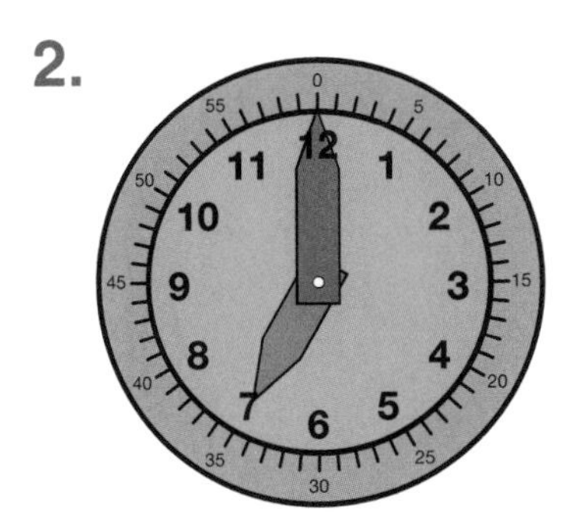

______

3.

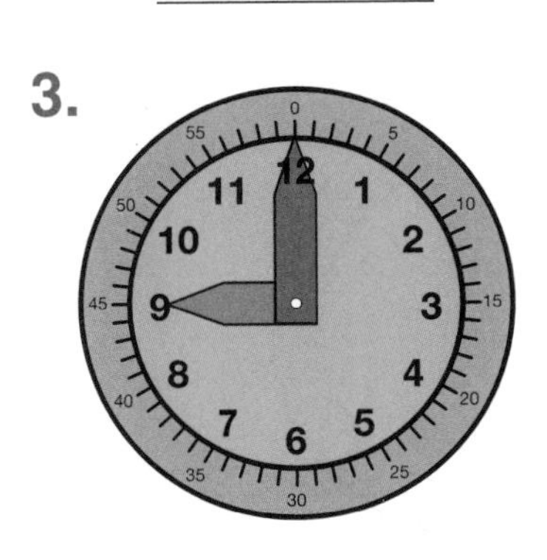

______

4.

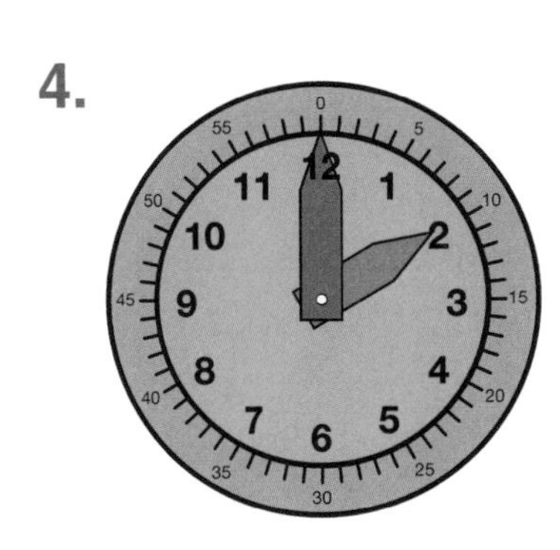

______

5.

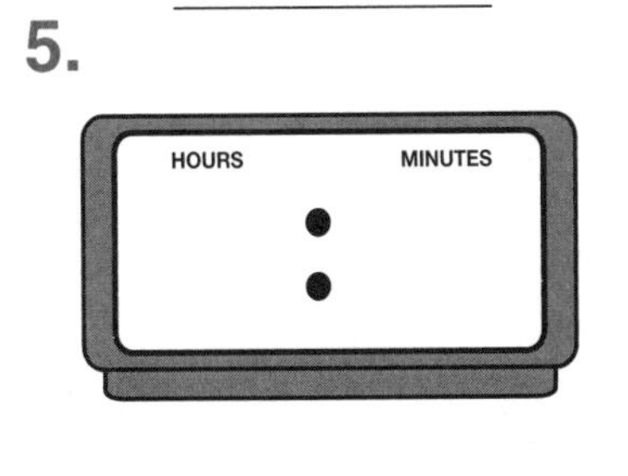

1:00

6.

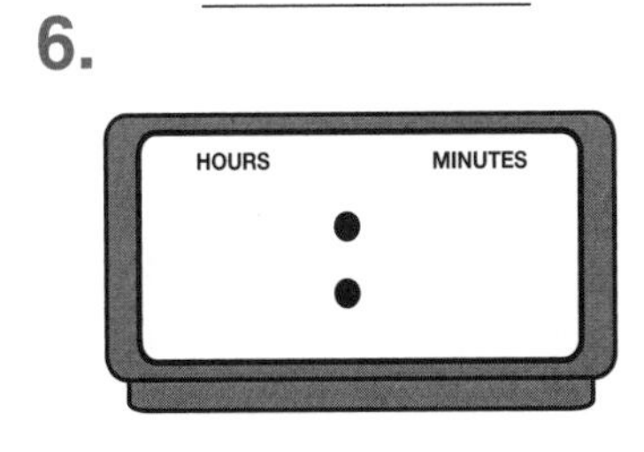

4:00

7.

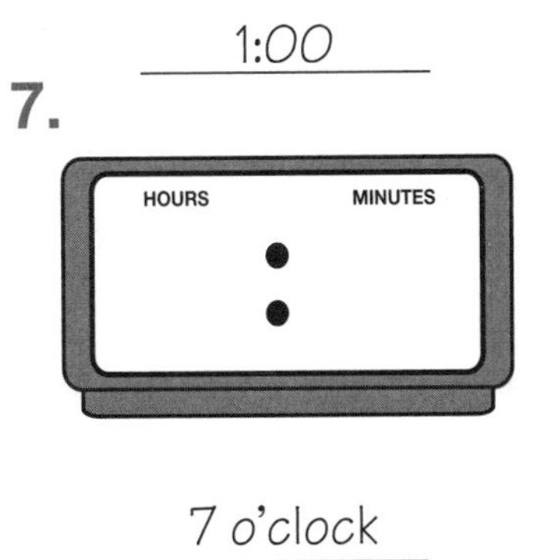

7 o'clock

8.

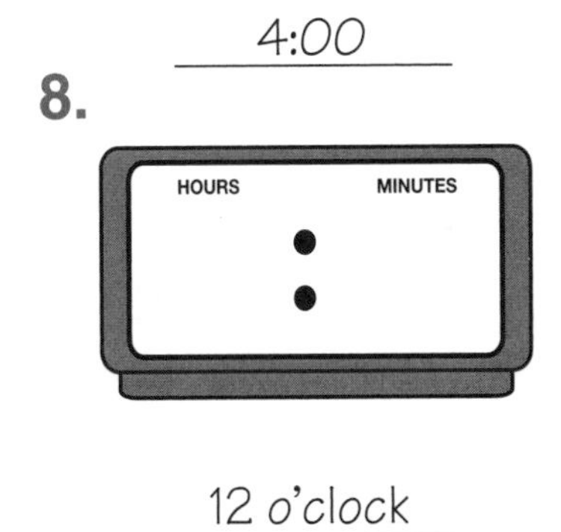

12 o'clock

Name ______________________ Date ______________

Just a Minute

Write the times on the clocks below.

1.

______

2.

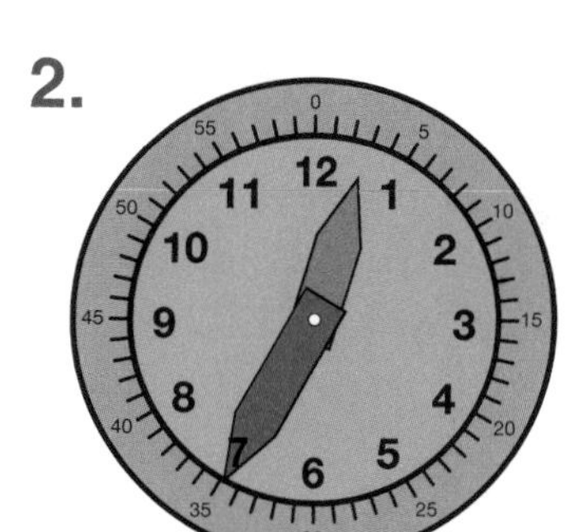

______

3.

______

4.

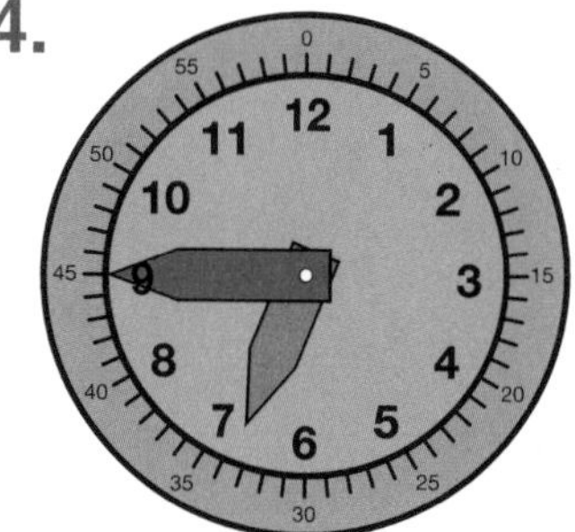

______

5.

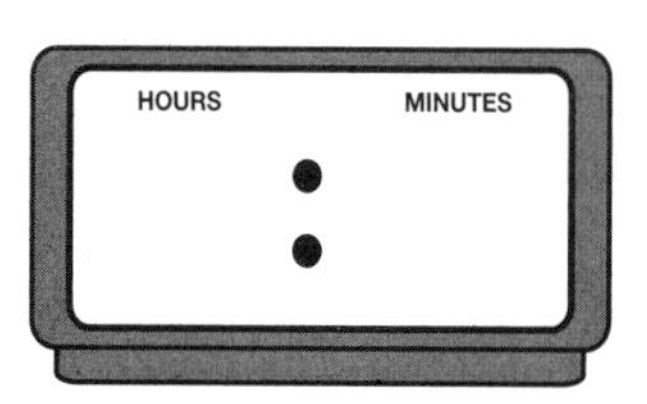

3:35

6.

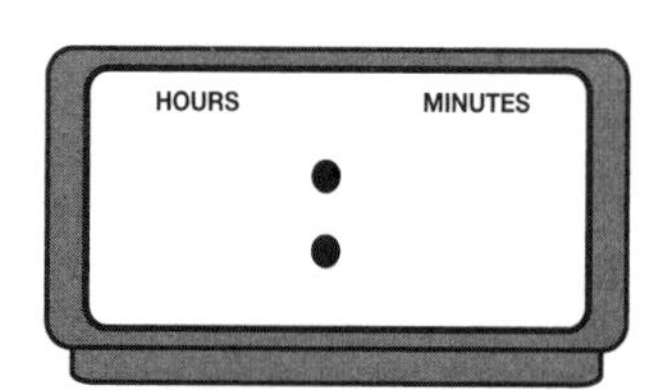

7:55

7.

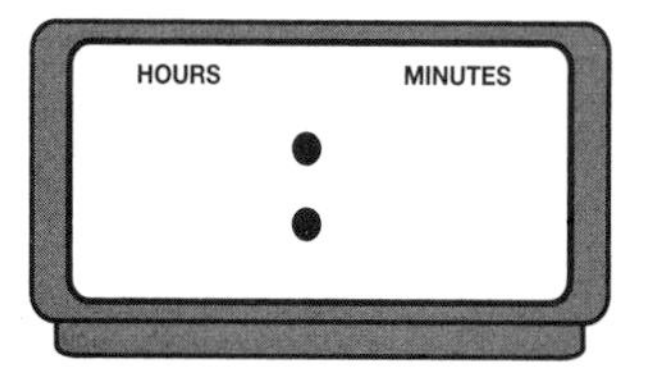

______

"It's four fifteen."

8.

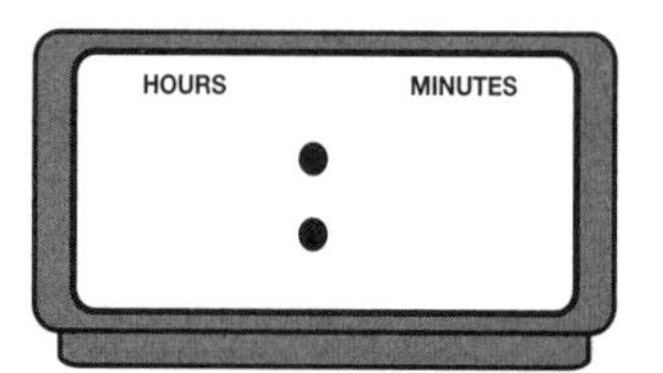

______

"It's nine twenty."

Name ______________________ Date ______________

Triangle Flash Cards: Group D

- Cut out the flash cards. To practice an addition fact, cover the corner with the highest number. (It is shaded.) Add the two uncovered numbers.
- Divide the cards into three piles: those facts you know and can answer quickly, those you can figure out with a strategy, and those you need to learn.
- Practice the last two piles again. Then make a list of the facts you need to practice at home.

Name ______________________ Date ______________

Group D

1 8 7 2 8 7 2 10 9

Group D

3 9 10 3 8 8 6 3 11 7 1 9

Group D

4 9 7 4 12 10 4 11 8

Name ________________________ Date __________

Place Value Mat

Name ______________________ Date ______________

Place Value Recording Sheet

Bundles of One Hundred	Stacks of Ten	Leftovers

Name ______________________ Date ______________

Professor Peabody's Problems

Solve the following problems with connecting cubes.

1. Nell and Ross each bought a bag of pasta. They used connecting cubes to show the number of pasta pieces in their bags.

Nell

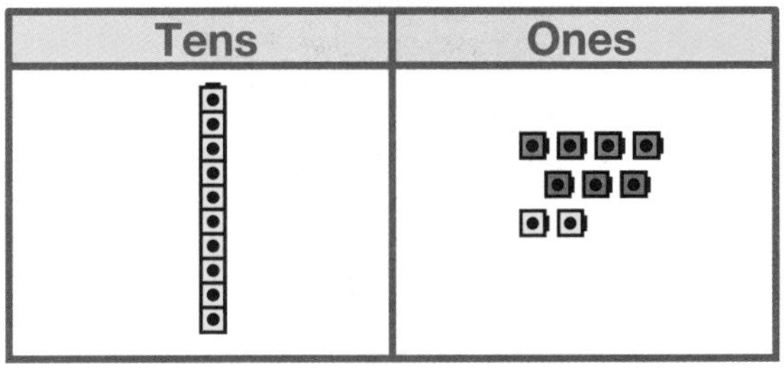

Tens	Ones

Ross

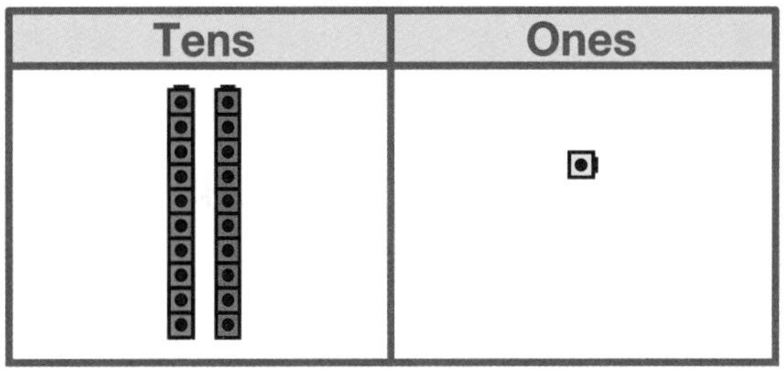

Tens	Ones

Professor Peabody said, "Nell's bag has more because it has nine loose cubes and Ross's only has one."

Is Professor Peabody right? ________
Explain how you know.

____

2. Clarissa has 32 pasta pieces. Melvin has 19. They showed their pieces with connecting cubes.

Clarissa

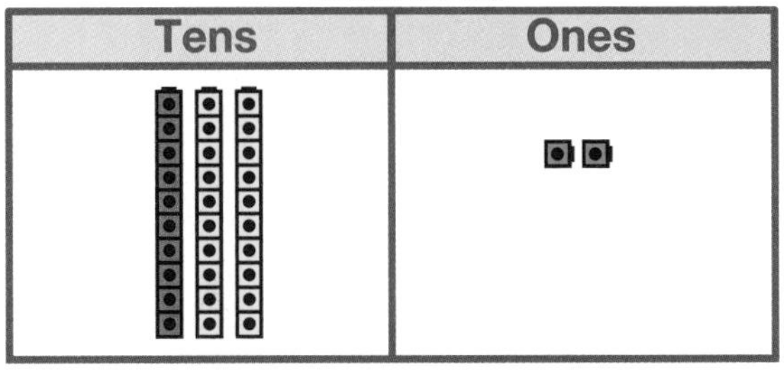

Tens	Ones

Melvin

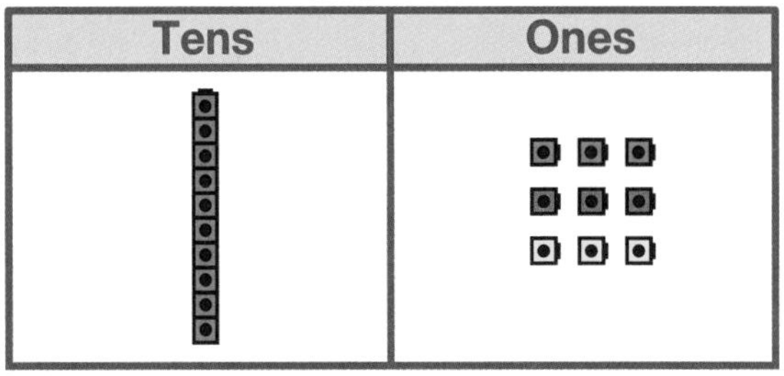

Tens	Ones

Professor Peabody said, "Melvin has more because he has 10 pieces and Clarissa only has 5." How would you help Professor Peabody? Explain.

____

Name ______________________ Date ____________

3. Tracy found a bag of pasta and wanted to model the number. There were 109 pieces in the bag. Professor Peabody used connecting cubes to model the number. Did Professor Peabody model 109 correctly?

____

Hundreds	Tens	Ones

Explain how you know.

____

Draw a correct model for 109 pieces.

Name ______________________ Date ______________

Not More Than 100

The goal of this game is to get as close to 100 cubes as possible in exactly five spins without going over.

Players

This is a game for two or more players.

Materials

- a pencil with paper clip for a spinner
- connecting cubes grouped in ones and tens

Rules

1. Make a chart like this one.
2. Spin five times. (All players share the same five spins.)
3. Each time the group spins, players take that number of ones or tens from the pile of cubes. Then players record the number taken on their charts.

   Example: A spin is 5. You can take 5 ones and record 5 **or** you can take 5 tens and record 50.
4. After five spins, the player who has the most connecting cubes, but not more than 100, wins.

My Score

Spin	Tens	Ones
1		
2		
3		
4		
5		
Total		

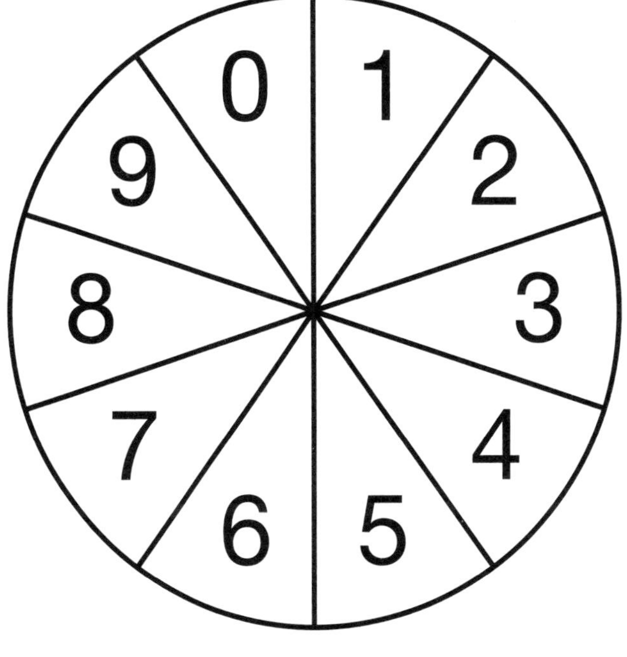

Name ______________________ Date ____________

Matching Cubes and Numbers

Homework

Dear Family Member:

Your child is learning about place value in class and using cubes to represent numbers. Help your child match the numbers and the pictures below.

Thank you for your cooperation.

Draw a line to match the models and the numbers.

1.

Bundles of 100	Stacks of 10	Leftovers
	1	2

2.

Bundles of 100	Stacks of 10	Leftovers
	3	6

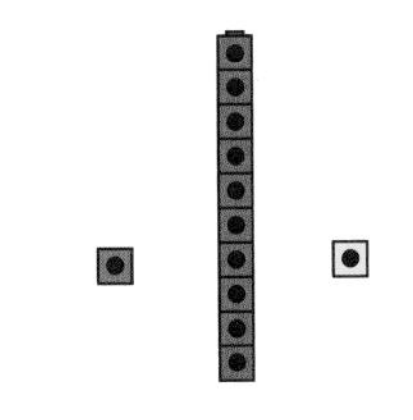

3.

Bundles of 100	Stacks of 10	Leftovers
	4	4

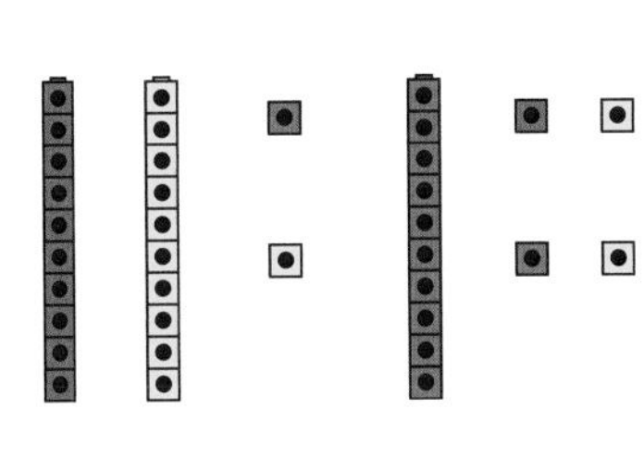

4.

Bundles of 100	Stacks of 10	Leftovers
1	2	9

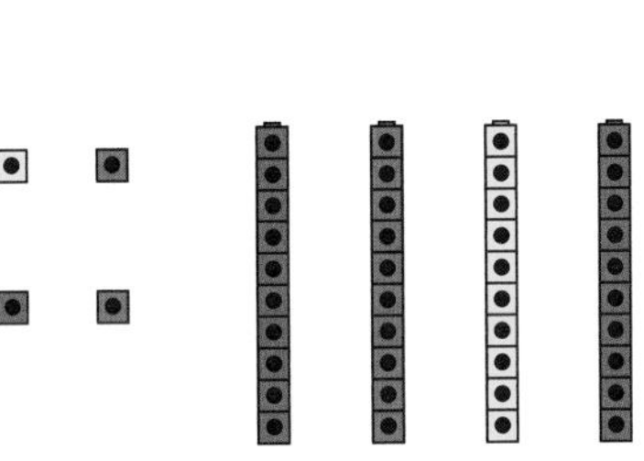

Name ______________________________ Date ______________

Draw pictures to represent the numbers.

5.

Bundles of 100	Stacks of 10	Leftovers
	1	5

6.

Bundles of 100	Stacks of 10	Leftovers
	2	3

Write the number shown in the picture.

7.

Bundles of 100	Stacks of 10	Leftovers

8.

Bundles of 100	Stacks of 10	Leftovers

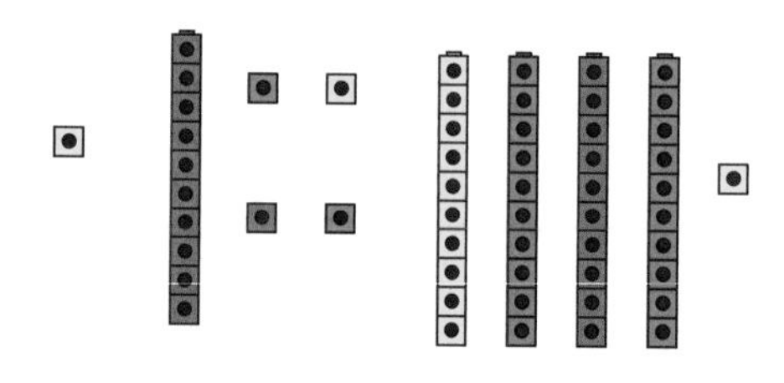

Name ______________________ Date ____________

Base-Ten Board

Flats	Skinnies	Bits

Name ______________________ Date ______________

Base-Ten Recording Sheet

Flats	Skinnies	Bits

Name ______________________ Date ______________

Base-Ten Numbers

Fill in the missing sections in the table.

	Number	One Way to Show Number
1.		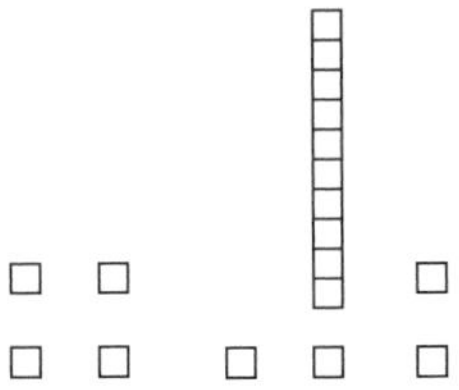
2.	23	
3.		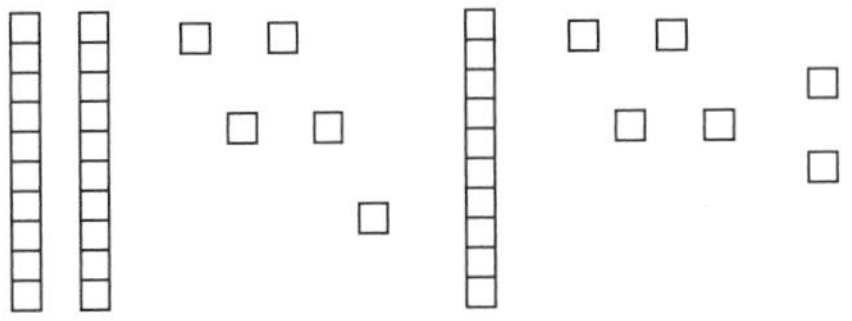
4.	85	
5.		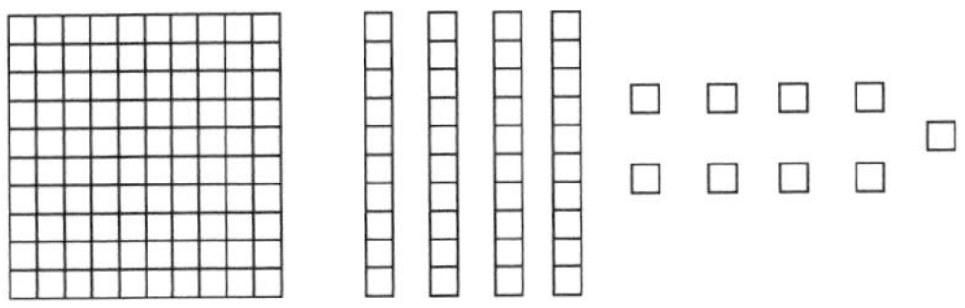

Name ______________________ Date ______________

Fill in the missing sections in the table.

	Number	One Way to Show Number
6.	111	
7.		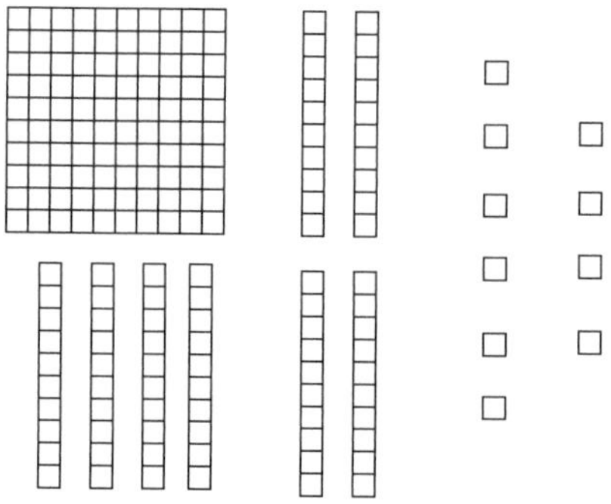
8.	303	
9.		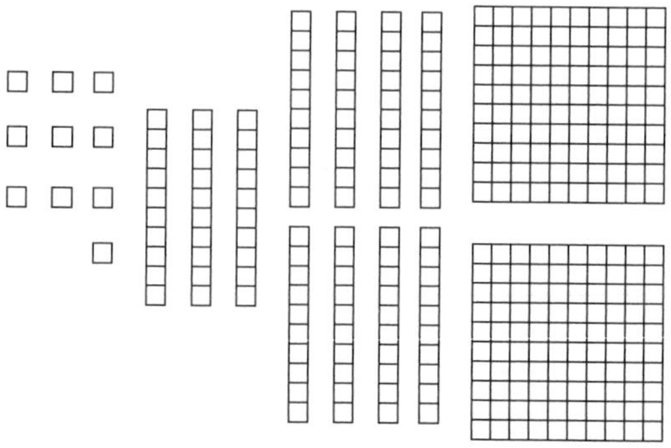

Name ______________________ Date ____________

Building Numbers

Dear Family Member:

Your child is learning about place value and using base-ten pieces to represent numbers. Ask your child to explain why both ways represent the same number in each problem.

Thank you for your help.

A number is shown with base-ten pieces. In each problem, name the number. Then write another way to make the number.

Example: **One Way**

Flats	Skinnies	Bits

Another Way

Flats	Skinnies	Bits
	11	13

Number 123

1. **One Way**

Flats	Skinnies	Bits

Another Way

Flats	Skinnies	Bits

Number ________

Name ______________________ Date ______________

2.

One Way

Flats	Skinnies	Bits

Another Way

Flats	Skinnies	Bits

Number ________

3.

One Way

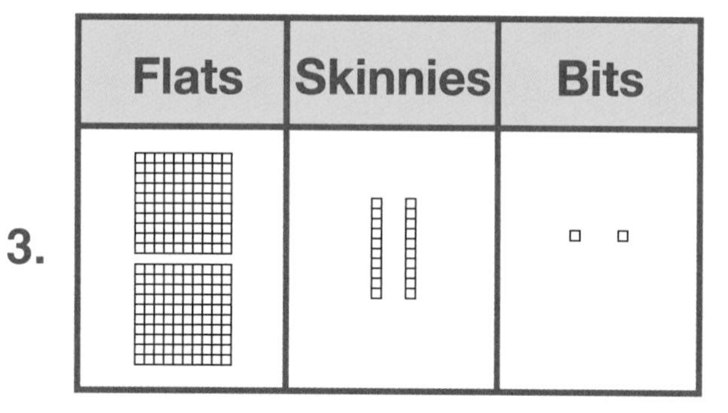

Flats	Skinnies	Bits

Another Way

Flats	Skinnies	Bits

Number ________

4.

One Way

Flats	Skinnies	Bits

Another Way

Flats	Skinnies	Bits

Number ________

Name ______________________ Date ______________

Take Your Places, Please

Players

This is a game for two players.

Materials

- *Take Your Places, Please Digit Mat*
- *Digit Cards*
- *Place Value Chart*

Rules

1. Agree with your partner to make the largest or the smallest number.
2. Draw the top card from your digit card deck.
3. Place the card in a frame on the digit mat.
4. Repeat steps 2 and 3 until you make a 3-digit number. You may put one card in the discard frame. But, once a card is on the mat, it cannot be moved.
5. Record the number on the *Place Value Chart*.
6. Compare your number with your partner's number.
7. The winner records a tally point on the *Place Value Chart*.
8. Play ten rounds and add up tally points.
9. The person with the most tallies wins!

Name ______________________ Date ______________

Take Your Places, Please Digit Mat

Place your digit cards on the frames below to make the largest or the smallest number.

Name ______________________ Date ______________

Digit Cards

Cut out the digit cards below.

4	9
3	8
2	7
1	6
0	5

Name ______________________ Date ______________

Place Value Chart

Record the numbers in the chart below. Mark a tally if you won the round.

Hundreds	Tens	Ones	Winning Tallies
		Total	

Name ______________________ Date ______________

Marshmallows and Containers

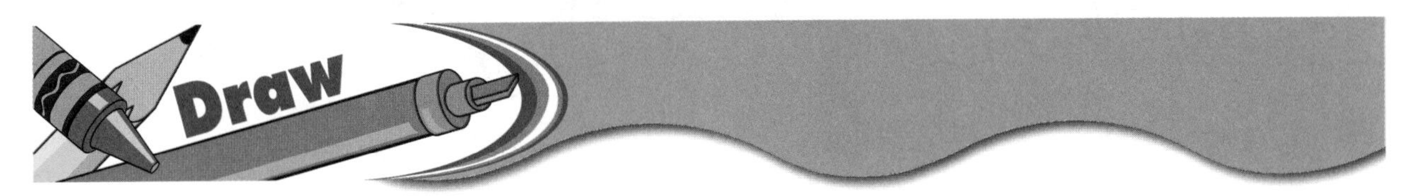

Draw a picture of the experiment setup. Be sure to include the two main variables.

C Container	*N* Number of ______ *unit*

Name ______________________ Date ______________

Make a graph of your data.

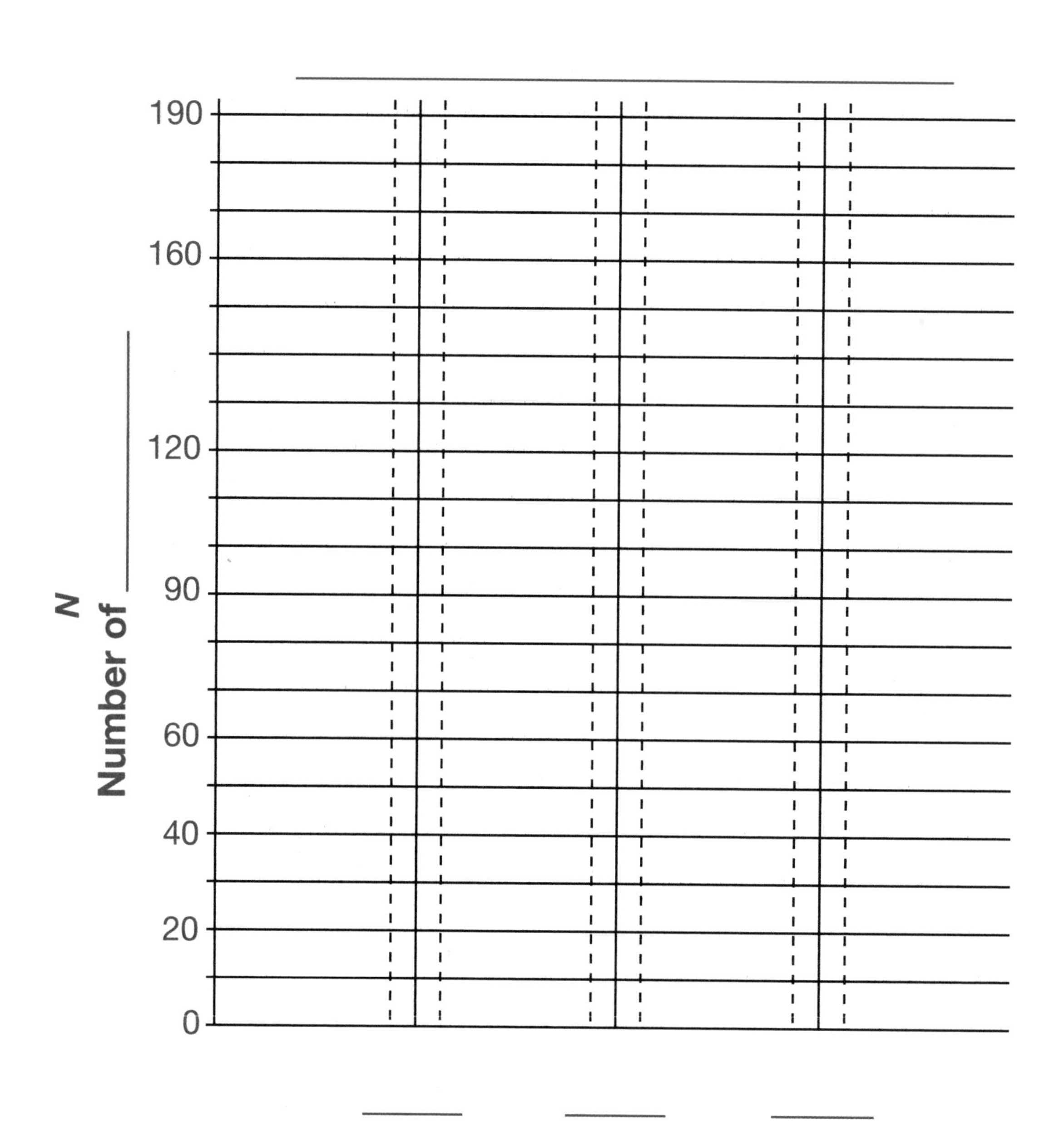

Name ______________________ Date ____________

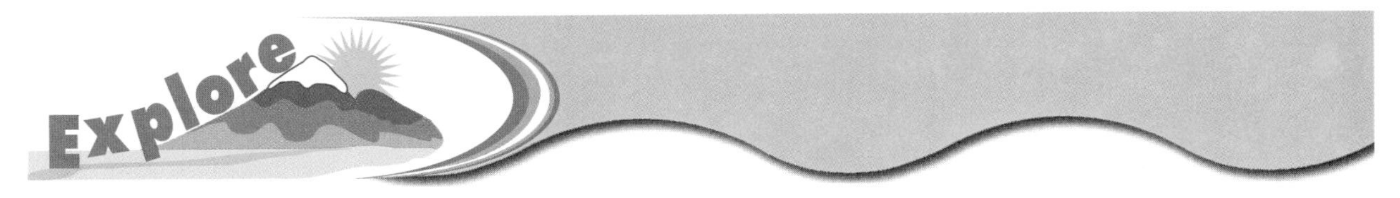

Use the data table and graph to answer the questions below.

1. What are the two main variables in this experiment?

   ____

2. Which container is the tallest? ____________

3. Which container is the widest? ____________

4. Which container holds the most marshmallows? How do you know?

   ____

   ____

5. Which container has the largest volume? How do you know?

   ____

   ____

6. Which container has the smallest volume? Explain your answer.

   ____

   ____

Name ______________________ Date ______________

Class Problem 1

Container D **Container E** **Container F**

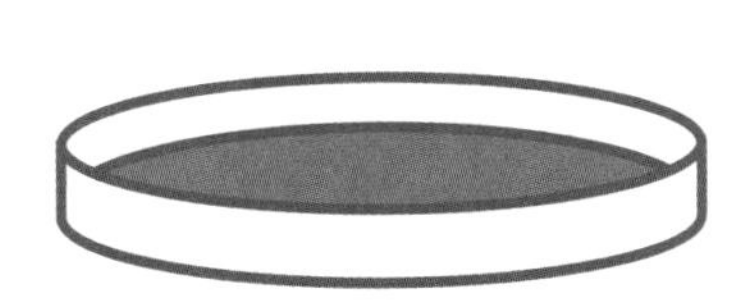

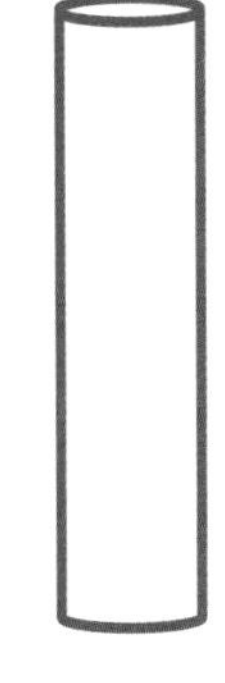

Container D holds 62 beans.

Container E holds 43 beans.

Container F holds 29 beans.

1. Which container has the largest volume?

____

2. Which container would hold the most water?

____

3. Suppose the beans from Container D are poured into empty Container F. Will all the beans fit?

____

If all the beans will not fit, how many beans will be left over? Tell how you know.

____

____

Name ______________________ Date ______________

Class Problem 2

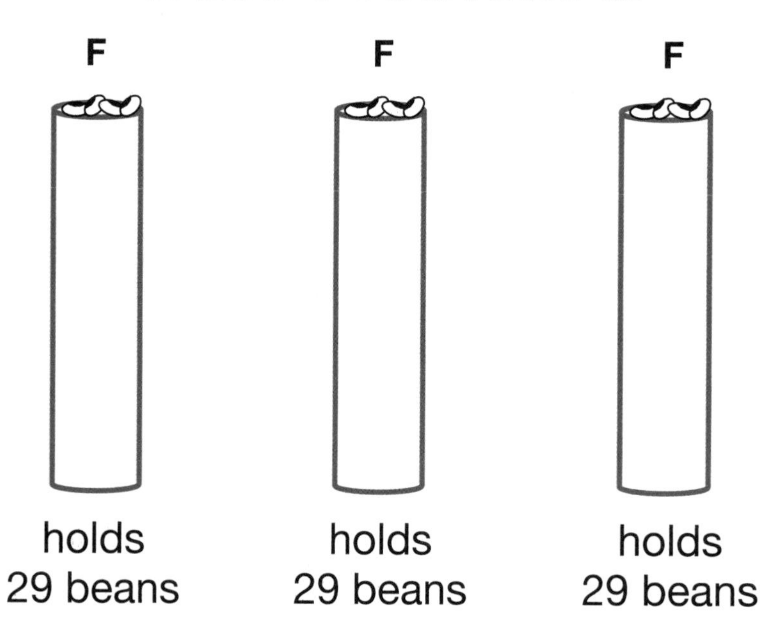

Container D
holds 62 beans.

Three F containers are filled with beans. Can an empty Container D hold all the beans? How can we find out?

____

____

____

____

Name ______________________ Date ______________

Partner Problems

Michael and Shenika collected the data below. Use their data to answer the following questions.

Marshmallows and Containers

C Container	*N* Number of Marshmallows (unit)
tall	103
medium	170
short	110

1. How many more marshmallows can the medium container hold than the tall container? Tell how you found your answer.

____

____

____

2. Can the beans from the tall and short containers fit into an empty medium container? Tell how you found your answer.

____

____

____

Unit 7

Building with Cubes

	Student Guide	Adventure Book	Unit Resource Guide*
Lesson 1			
Cubes and Plans	●		
Lesson 2			
Cube Model Plans	●		●
Lesson 3			
Architects in Cubeland	●		●
Lesson 4			
3-D Building Plans	●		●
Lesson 5			
Cube Model Problems	●		

***Unit Resource Guide* pages are from the teacher materials.**

Name ______________________ Date ______________

Cube Model Pictures

Use words and pictures to show each shape you made using four connecting cubes.

Name ______________________ Date ______________

Cube Model Twins

Look at the drawings of the cube models below. For each problem, circle the two drawings that have the *same shape.*

1. 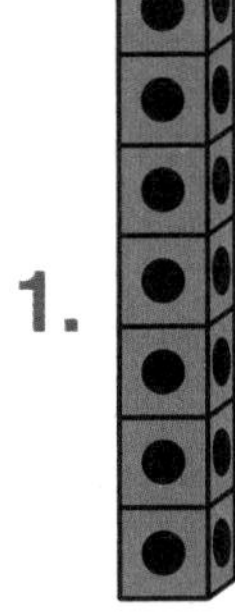 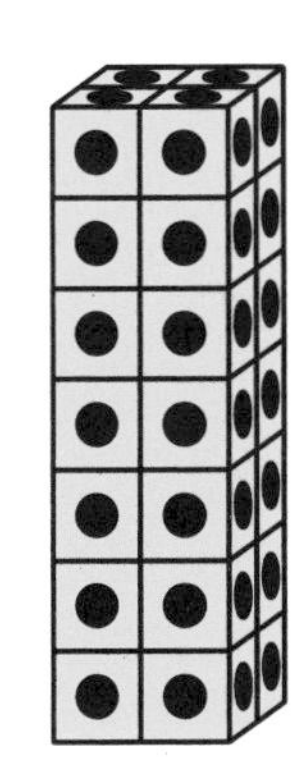  

2.    

3. 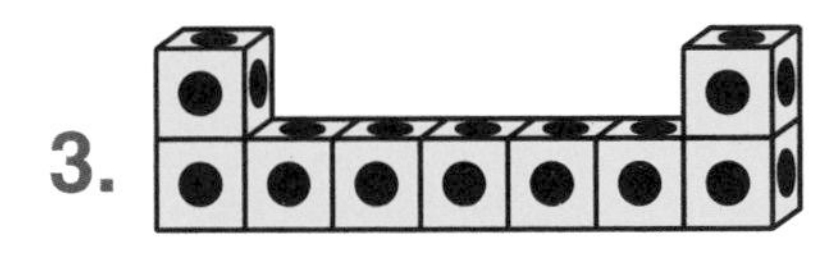   

Name ________________________ Date ________________

Triangle Flash Cards: Group E

- Cut out the flash cards. To practice an addition fact, cover the corner with the highest number. (It is shaded.) Add the two uncovered numbers.
- Divide the cards into three piles: those facts you know and can answer quickly, those you can figure out with a strategy, and those you need to learn.
- Practice the last two piles again. Then make a list of the facts you need to practice at home.

Name ______________________________ Date ______________

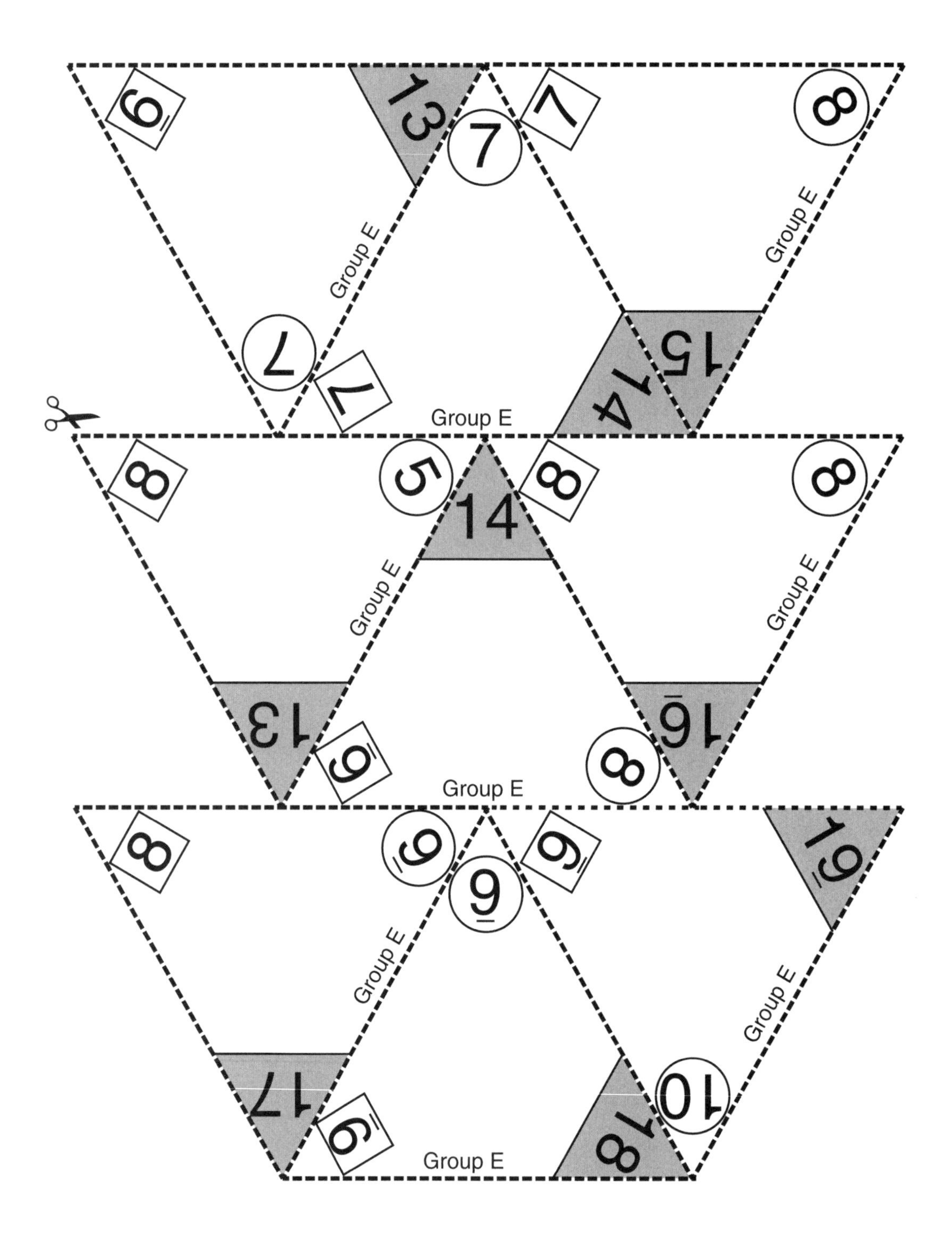

6
13
7
7
8
Group E
Group E
7
7
15
14
Group E
8
5
14
8
8
Group E
Group E
13
6
16
8
Group E
8
6
6
6
19
Group E
Group E
17
6
18
10
Group E

Name ______________________ Date ______________

Sarah's Cube Models

Sarah made two cube models. Her plans are below.

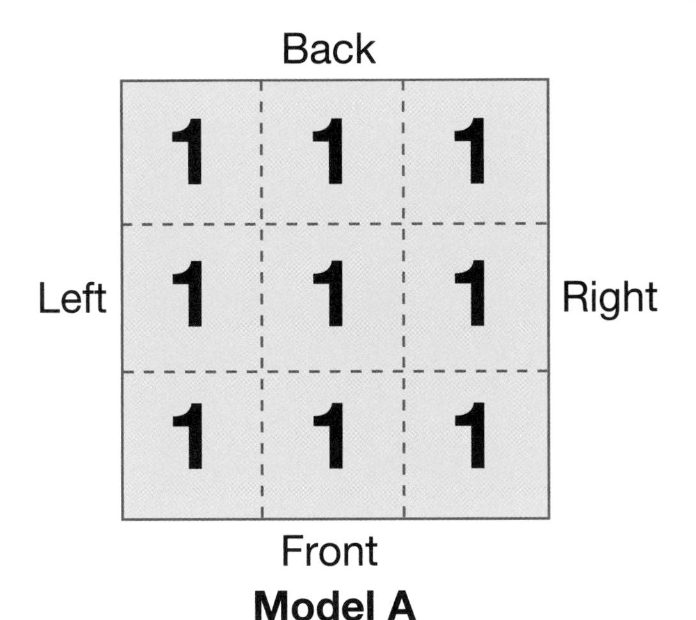

Model A

Back

	2	2
	2	2

Left / Right

Front

Model B

Make Sarah's cube models using her plans.

Which model do you think is the biggest? Explain why.

____

____

____

____

____

____

____

____

____

Name ______________________ Date ______________

Sarah and Sebastian's Cube Tower Plan

Sarah and Sebastian used cubes to make a tower.

Write two different number sentences that describe the volume in cubic units.

____

____

Back

4	2	1
2	2	1
1	1	1

Left — Right

Front

Name ______________________ Date ______________

Galen's Cube Tower Plan

Use the plan below to build a tower that looks like the one Galen built.

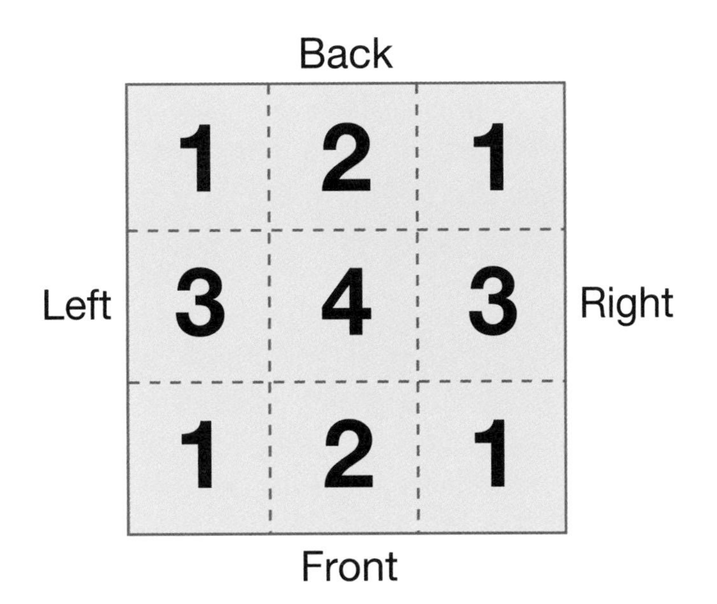

1. Ask your teacher to show you a model of Galen's tower. Does it look like yours?

____

2. What is the volume of your tower?

____

3. Write a number sentence to describe the volume in cubic units.

____

____

Name ______________________ Date ______________

What If Volume Problems

Dear Family Member:

Your child is learning to build cube models and describe them using plans. Have your child describe what the numbers in the grid represent.

Thank you.

Below are the cube model plans you used to build two towers.

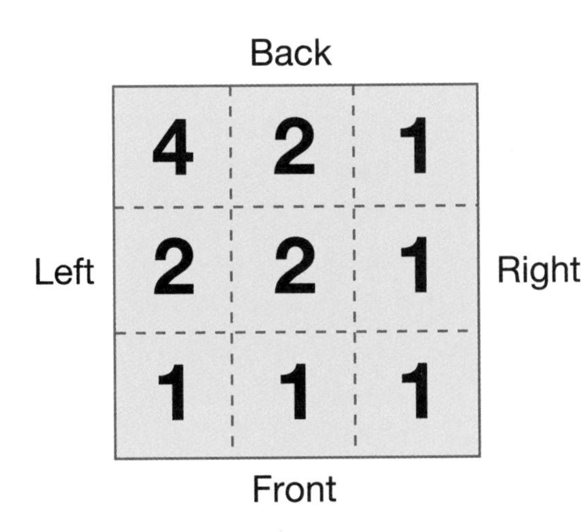

Sarah and Sebastian's Cube Model Plan

1. What is the volume of this model? ______________
2. What if Sarah and Sebastian added one story to each column of their building? What will the new volume be?

   ______________ Write a number sentence to describe the new volume in cubic units. ______________
3. What if they made all the columns the same height as the tallest column? Write a number sentence to describe this volume in cubic units. ______________

Name ______________________ Date ______________

Below is Galen's Cube Model Plan.

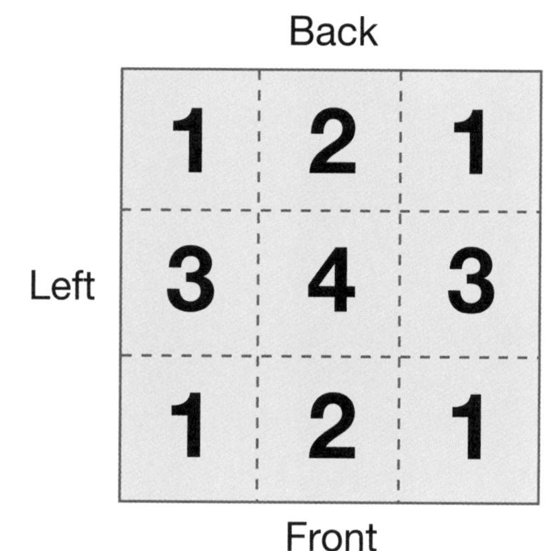

Galen's Cube Model Plan

4. What is the volume of this model? ______________
5. What if Galen added two stories to each column of his building? What would the new volume be?

   ______________ Write a number sentence to describe the new volume in cubic units. ______________
6. What if the center column of Galen's building was seven stories high instead of four stories high? Write a number sentence to describe this volume in cubic units.

   ____

Name ______________________ Date ______________

Cubeland Memo

Construct a building with cubes, and then make a plan.

Write a memo describing your new building to another architect team. Use the questions to write a description.

- How tall is the building?
- How long is the building from front to back?
- How many cubes make up the building?

Exchange the memo and your cube model plan with another team. Use the memo and the cube model plan to make a building that looks like the one that the other team built.

MEMO

TO: ______________________
names of student architects

FROM: ______________________
names of student architects

DATE: ______________________
month, day, year

Here is our team's description of our new building:

____

____

____

Name ______________________ Date ______________

What's the Volume?

Find the volume for the cube model plans and buildings.

1. 

_____ cubic units

2. 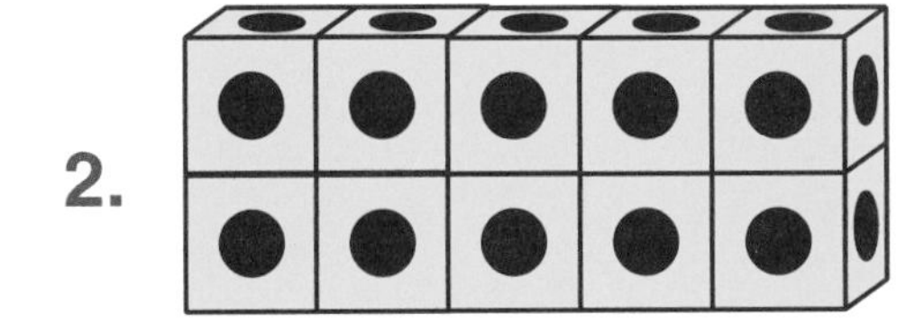

_____ cubic units

3.

Back

Left

4	4	2
2	4	4

Right

Front

_____ cubic units

4.

Back

Left

8	1
12	9

Right

Front

_____ cubic units

Name ______________________ Date ______________

City Buildings

Build cube models that look like the three drawings below. Find the volume of each building and write a number sentence to show your strategy.

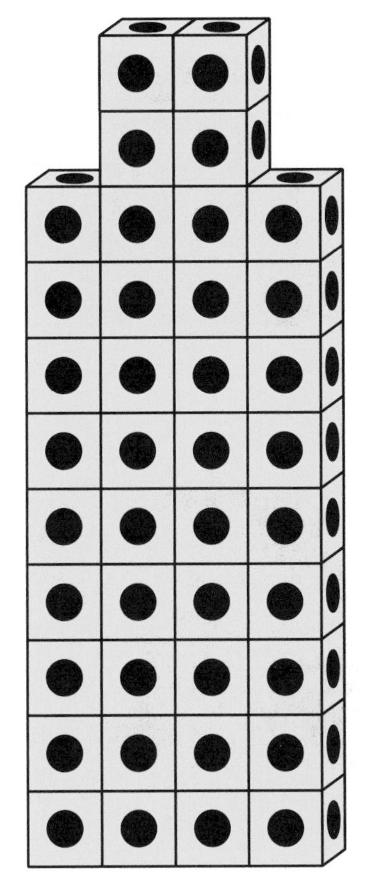

A. Quad City Towers

Volume ________

Number sentence ______________

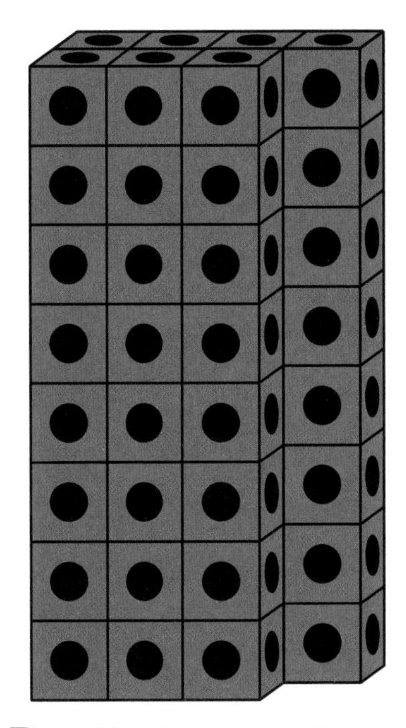

B. Six Corners Gym

Volume ________

Number sentence ______________

Volume ________

Number sentence ______________

C. Stair Step Apartments

Name ______________________________ Date ________________

City Buildings Match-Up

Which cube model goes with which cube plan? Draw a line from the plan to the matching model. Explain how you know.

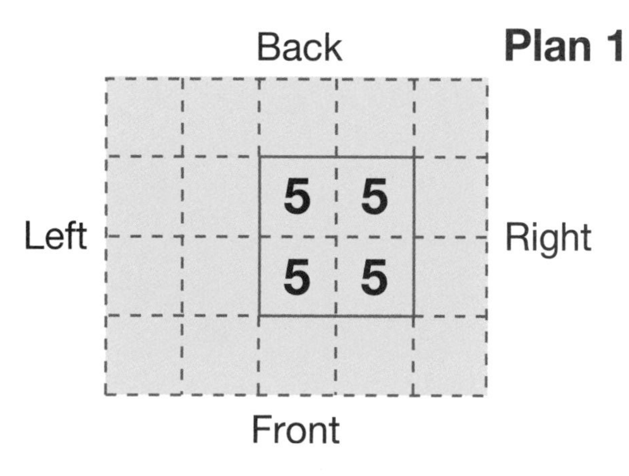

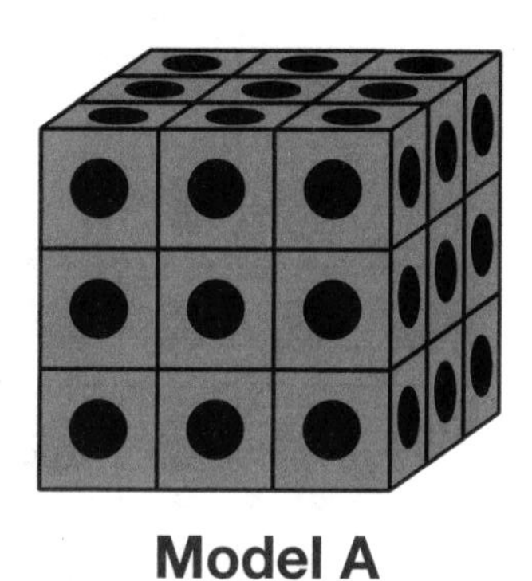

Model A

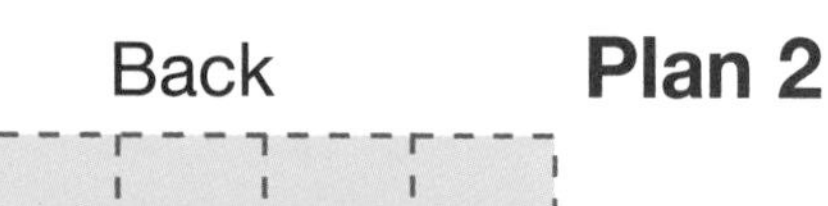

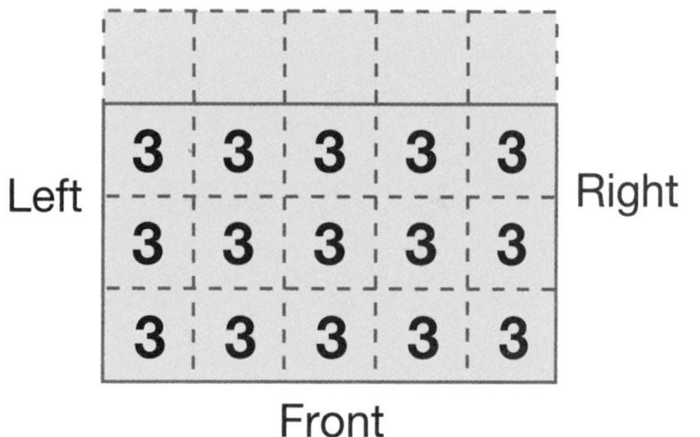

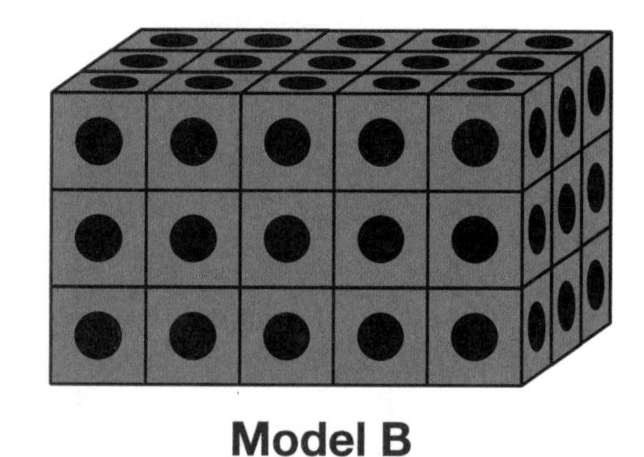

Model B

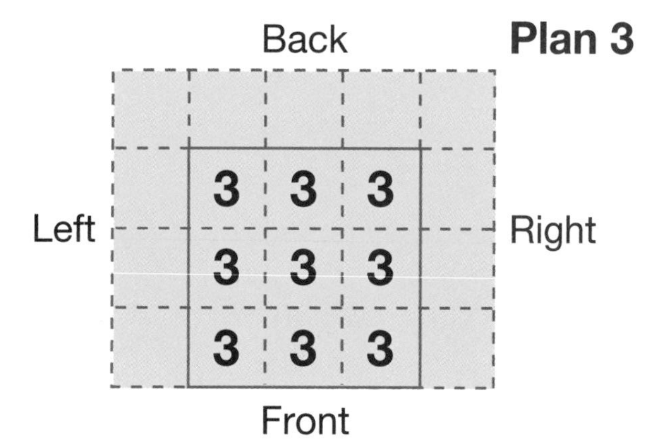

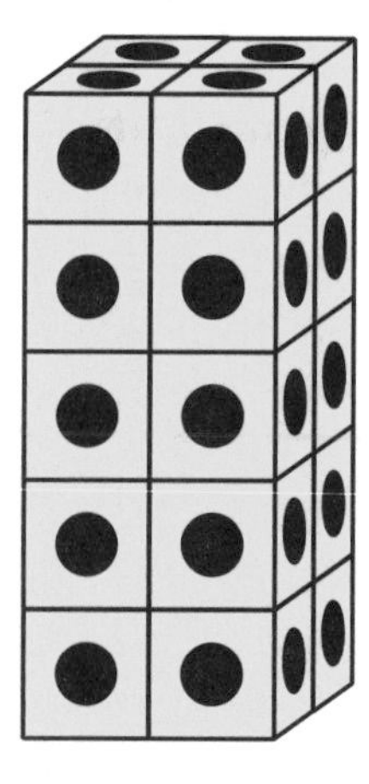

Model C

Name ______________________ Date ______________

Matching Plans with Models 1

Match the plan with the model, and connect them with a line. Find the volume of each model. Explain how you know.

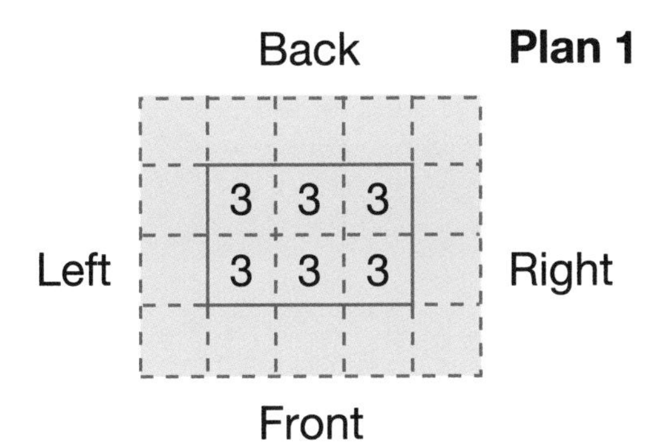

Model A

Volume ________

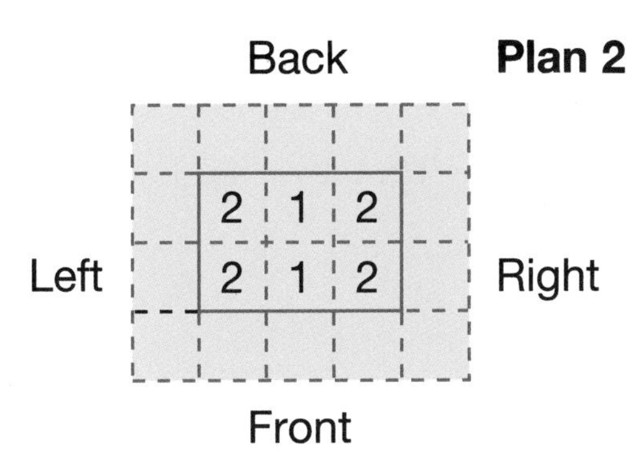

Model B

Volume ________

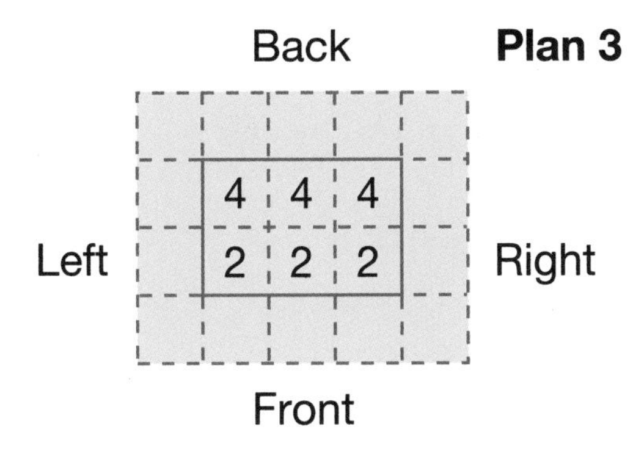

Model C

Volume ________

Name ______________________ Date ______________

Matching Plans with Models 2

Draw a line from the plan to the matching model. Find the volume of each model.

Back **Plan 1**

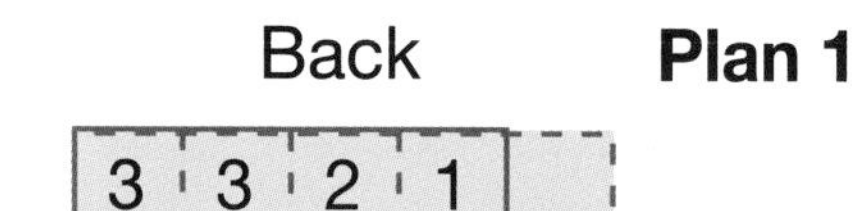

Left

3	3	2	1
2	2	2	1
1	1	1	1

Right

Front

Model A

Volume ________

Back **Plan 2**

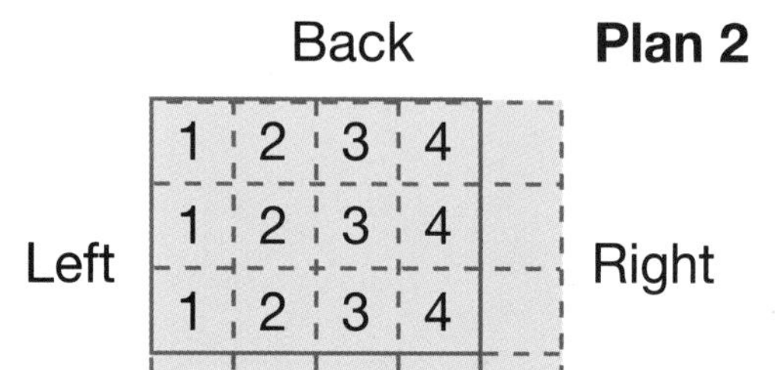

Front

Model B

Volume ________

Back **Plan 3**

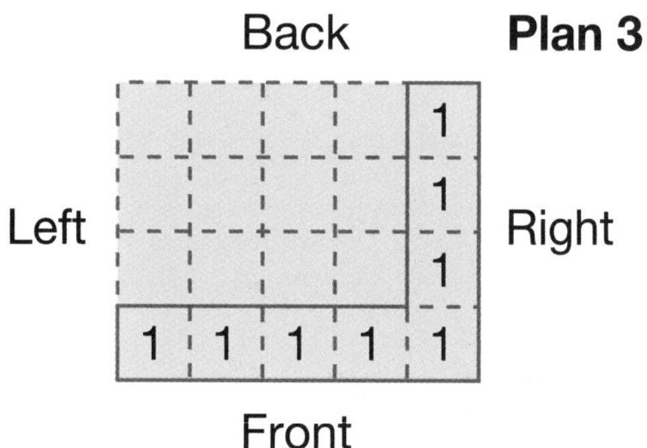

Front

Model C

Volume ________

Name ______________________ Date ______________

Cube Model Problems

1. Use the following floor plans to make a cube model building with:

A. 9 cubes

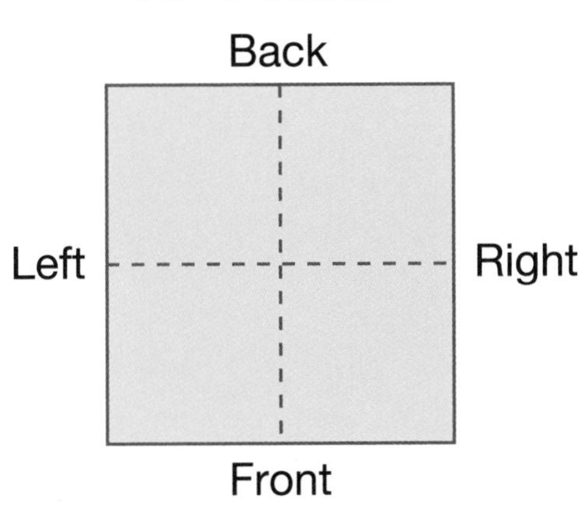

B. 11 cubes

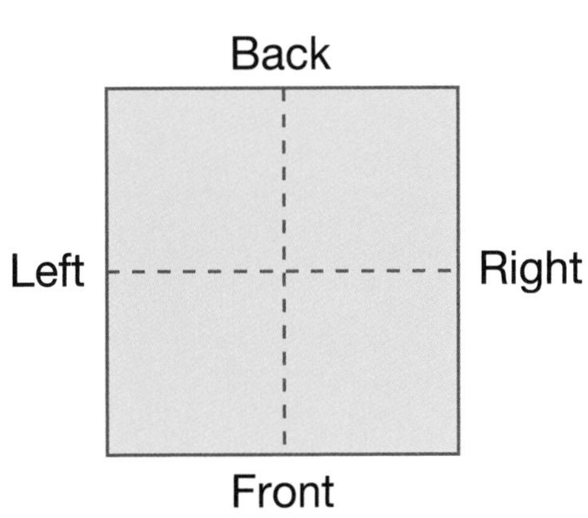

C. 16 cubes

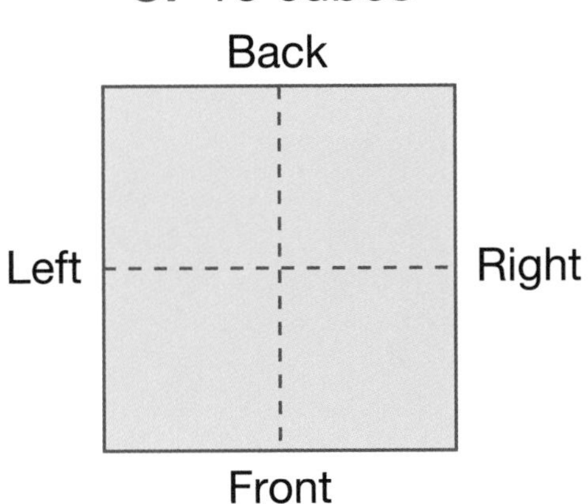

2. Use the following floor plan to make a building out of 9 cubes.

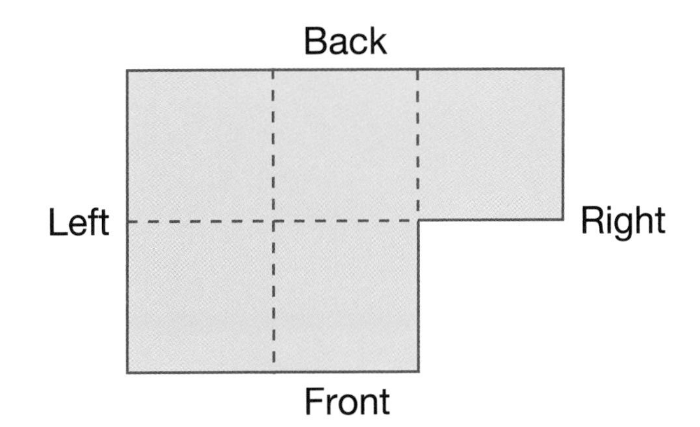

Name ______________________ Date ______________

More Cube Model Problems

Work with a partner. Build a cube model that matches the clues in each problem. Make a record of your model on the cube model plan. You may find no solutions, one solution, or many solutions.

1. **Clues**
   - The floor plan is a square with each side 2 units long.
   - Volume = 8 cubic units
   - Height = 2 units

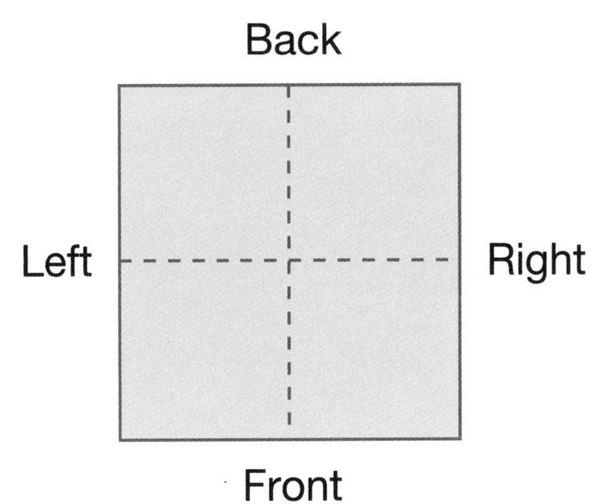

2. **Clues**
   - The floor plan is a square with each side 2 units long.
   - Volume = 6 cubic units
   - Height = 2 units

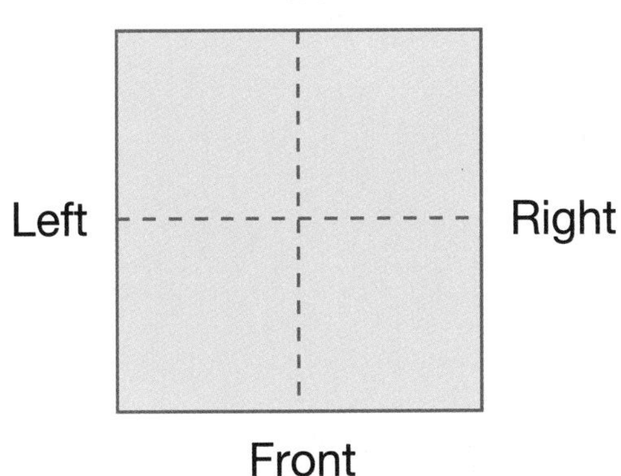

3. **Clues**
   - The floor plan is a square with each side 2 units long.
   - Volume = 9 cubic units
   - Height = 2 units

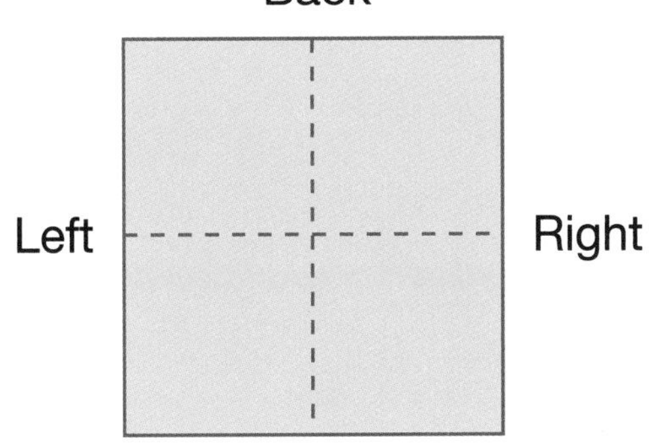

Name ______________________ Date ______________

4. **Clues**

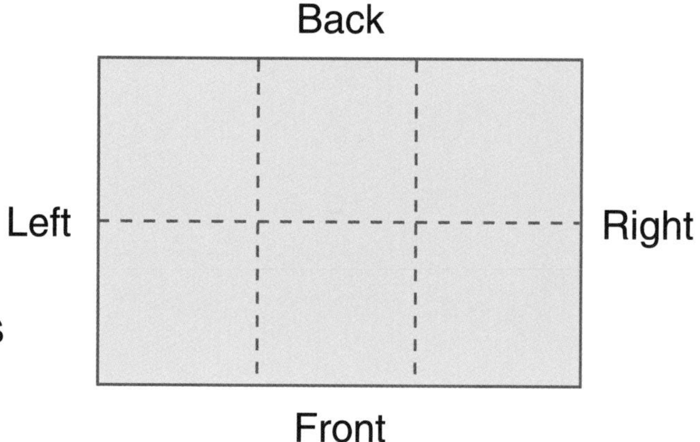

- The floor plan is a rectangle that is 3 units long and 2 units wide.
- Volume = 7 cubic units
- Height = 2 units

5. Make up your own cube model problem. Make sure you know the answer.

Clues

- The floor plan is a rectangle that is _____ units long

  and _____ units wide.

- Volume = _____ • Height = _____

6. Which problems have only one solution? Circle them.

Problem number	1	2	3	4

7. Which problems have more than one solution? Circle them.

Problem number	1	2	3	4

8. Which problems have no solution? Circle them.

Problem number	1	2	3	4

Name ______________________ Date ______________

Cube Model Challenge

Homework

Dear Family Member:

Your child is learning to build cube models and describe them using plans. Ask your child how he or she recorded plans in class. It will help if you imagine placing each 3-dimensional model on the grid.

Thank you for your cooperation.

Make a cube model plan from the drawing, *without using the cubes.*

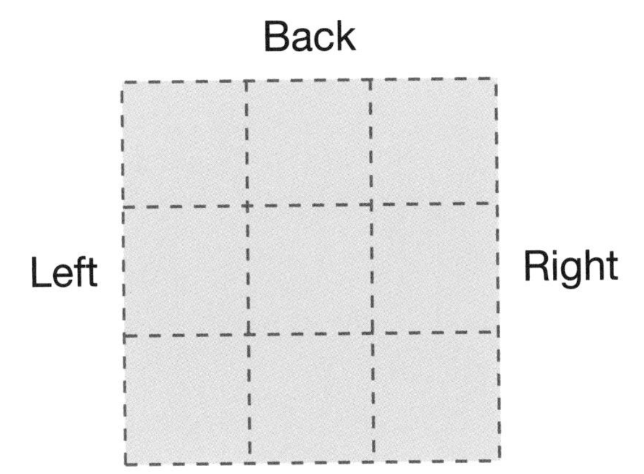

Volume = _____

Volume = _____

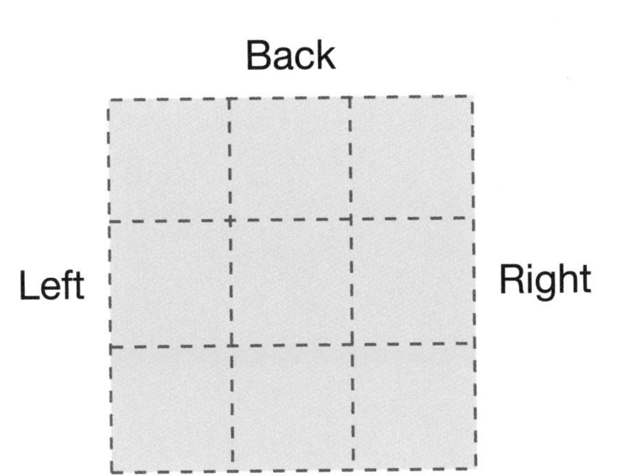

Name ______________________ Date ______________

Give Me a Clue

Read the clues for each problem. Build a cube model that solves each problem. Make a record of your model on the cube model plan.

1. **Clues**
   - The floor plan is a square with each side 2 units long.
   - Volume = 7 cubic units
   - Height = 4 units

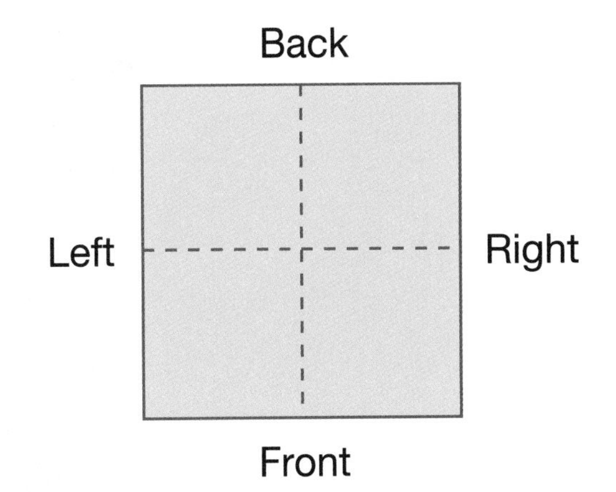

2. **Clues**
   - The floor plan is a square with each side 2 units long.
   - Volume = 10 cubic units
   - Height = 3 units

Back

Left

Right

Front

3. **Clues**
   - The floor plan is shown at the right.
   - Volume = 6 cubic units
   - Height = 2 units

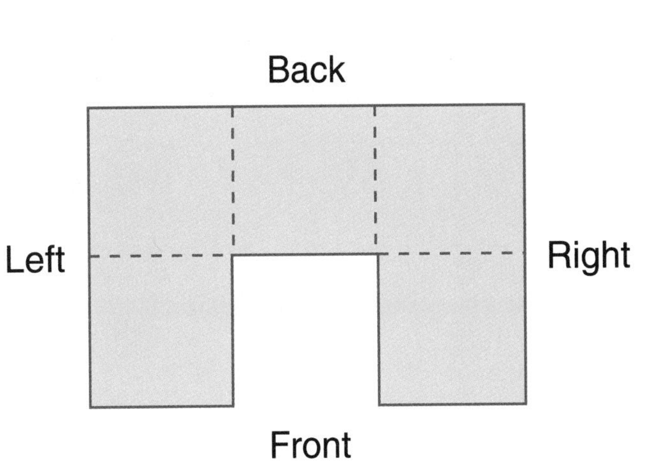

Unit 8

Multiple Masses

	Student Guide	Adventure Book	Unit Resource Guide*
Lesson 1			
Putting Masses in Order	●		
Lesson 2			
The Mouse-Proof Shelf	●	●	
Lesson 3			
Measuring Mass	●		●

***Unit Resource Guide* pages are from the teacher materials.**

Name ________________________ Date ______________

Comparing Masses

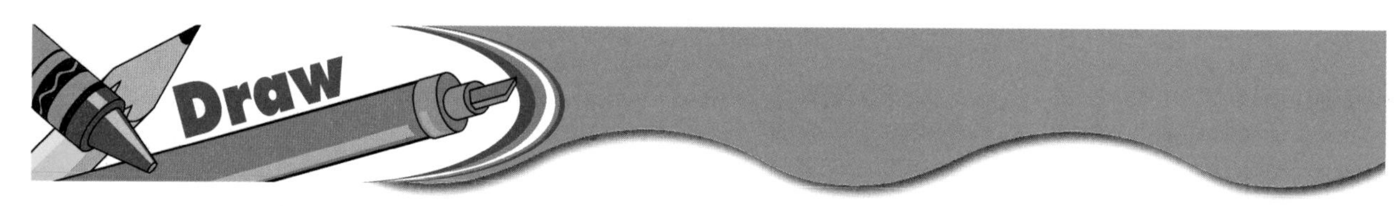

Predict and line up objects from most mass to least mass. Draw and label the order of your objects.

Compare masses on the two-pan balance. Record your results in the table.

Mass Comparison Data Table

Object in Pan 1	Object in Pan 2	More Mass

Name ______________________ Date ______________

Analyzing Masses

Decide on the order of masses. Then fill in the table below.

Mass Order Data Table

Mass Order	Name of Object
Most Mass	
↓	
↓	
Least Mass	

1. Which objects are the same size and shape?

   ____

2. Do these two objects have the same mass? Why?

   ____

3. Are the wood and steel spheres the same shape?

   ____

4. Which is smaller: the wood or steel sphere? ______________

Name ______________________ Date ______________

5. Which has more mass: the wood or steel sphere? __________

6. Two new spheres are shown below. Which has more mass?

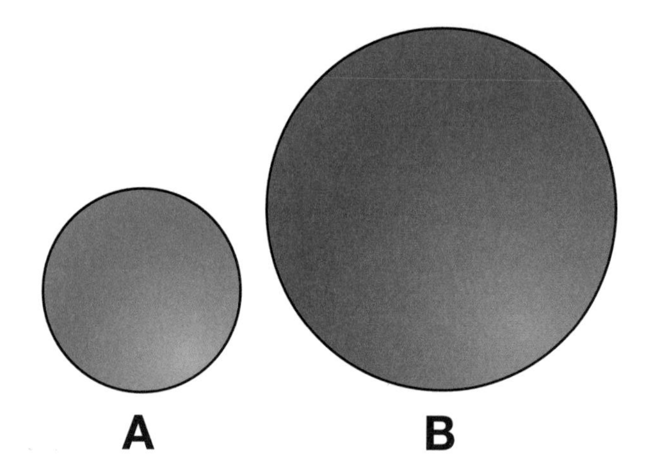

Explain.

____

____

____

____

---

7. Cylinder A and Cylinder B are the same shape and size.

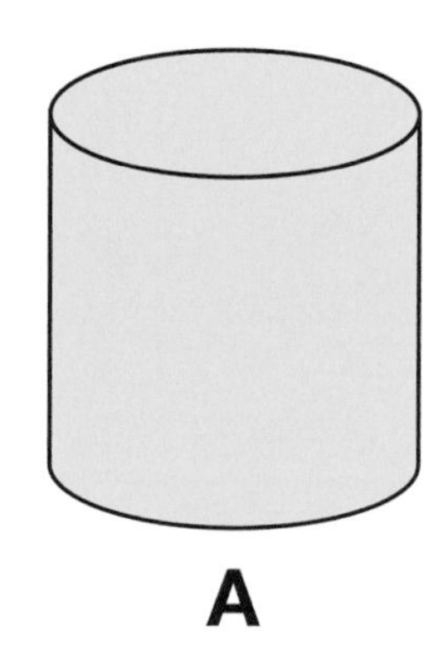

B

Mark the correct statement below.

__________ The masses are the same.

__________ Cylinder B has more mass.

__________ Cylinder A has more mass.

__________ You can't tell which has more mass.

Name ______________________ Date ______________

Mass Hunt

Dear Family Member:

Your child is learning to find and compare the masses (weights) of objects. Help your child search for two small objects at home that have similar masses (weights), but different shapes or sizes. (Note: Objects that have the same weights will also have the same masses.)

Thank you for your cooperation.

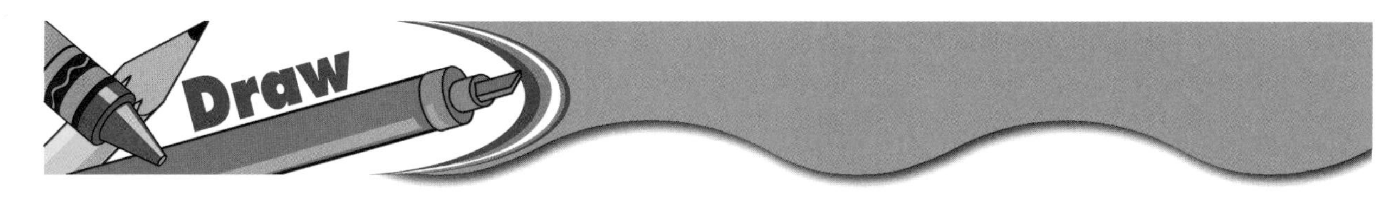

Draw the objects below. Tell how you predict they have the same mass.

____

____

____

Bring the two objects to school. Check your predictions using the two-pan balance.

Name ______________________ Date ______________

Analyzing the Masses of Two Blocks

Here is a picture of two objects.

1. Do the objects have the same shape?

   ____

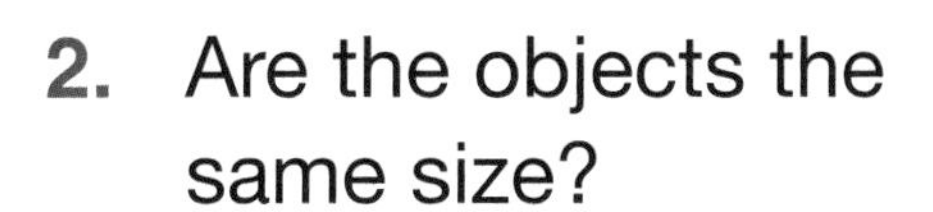

2. Are the objects the same size?

   ____

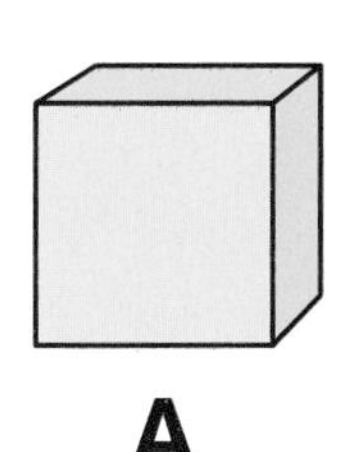

A

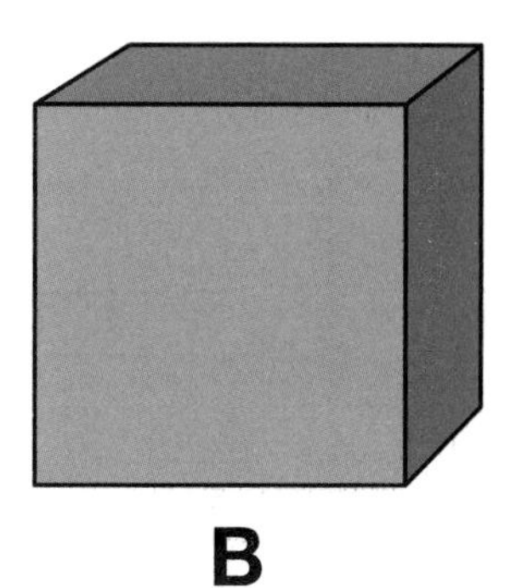

B

3. Can you tell which one has more mass? Explain.

   ____

   ____

4. Block A and Block B are put on the balance. Does one of the pictures below show what will happen? Circle that picture.

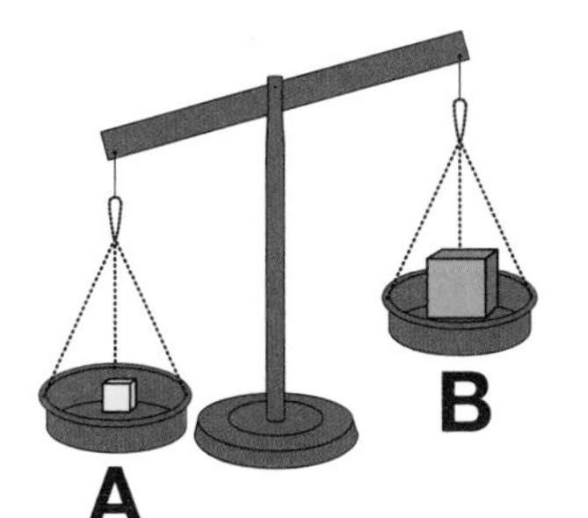

Picture 1

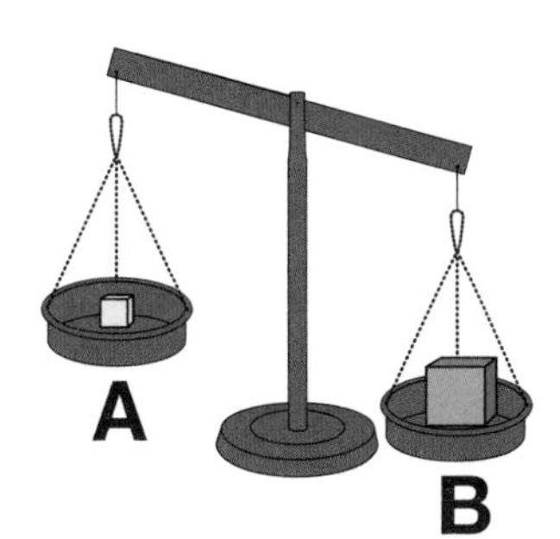

Picture 2

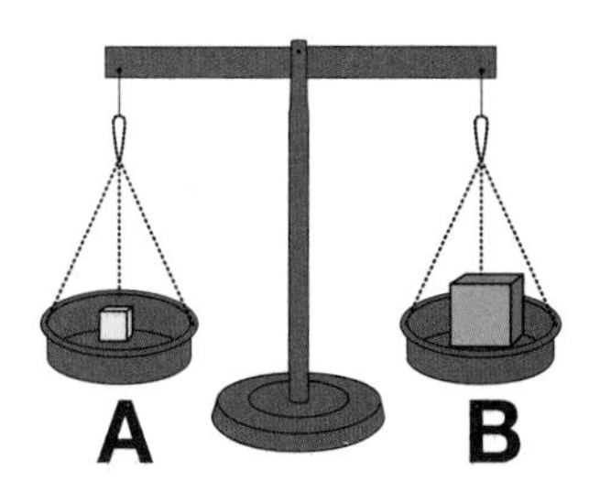

Picture 3

________ I can't tell what will happen.

Name ______________________________ Date ________________

Triangle Flash Cards: Group F

- Cut out the flash cards. To practice an addition fact, cover the corner with the highest number. (It is shaded.) Add the two uncovered numbers.
- Divide the cards into three piles: those facts you know and can answer quickly, those you can figure out with a strategy, and those you need to learn.
- Practice the last two piles again. Then make a list of the facts you need to practice at home.

Name ______________________ Date ______________

Group F

Group F

Group F

Group F

Group F

Group F

Group F

Group F

Name ________________________ Date ________________

Millie, Minnie, Marty, and Mike Did It!

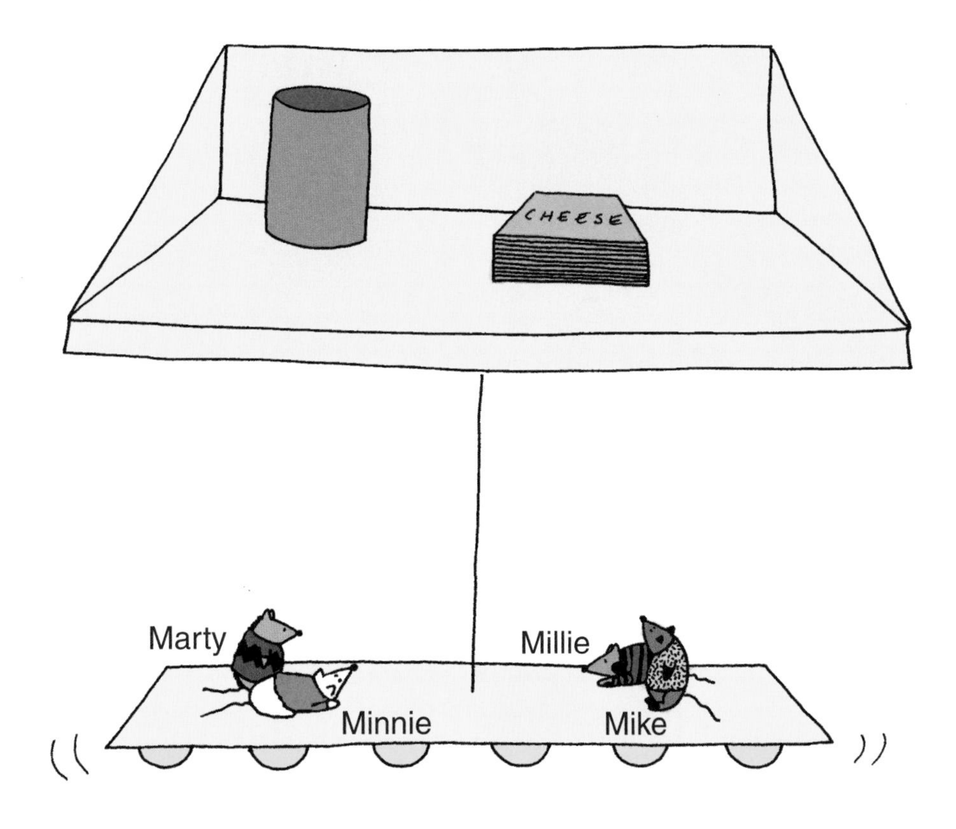

Marty and Minnie are on one side of the lamp. Millie and Mike are on the other side. The lamp is balanced! What could be the masses of the four mice?

Work with a partner. Pretend the mice can have any of these masses: 9 grams, 8 grams, 7 grams, 6 grams, 5 grams, 4 grams, 3 grams, 2 grams, or 1 gram. Each mouse has a different mass.

You can use connecting cubes to represent each mouse's mass. Check your combinations on the two-pan balance.

Record the combinations of masses in the tables on the next page.

Name ______________________ Date ______________

Millie's and Mike's total mass should equal Minnie's and Marty's total mass. The first row shows an example.

Mouse Masses in Grams

Marty	Minnie	Total
4	5	9

Millie	Mike	Total
8	1	9

Name ______________________ Date ______________

Measuring Mass

Draw a picture of the lab. Include the two main variables and the materials you will use.

Before you collect data, what must you do to the balance?

____

Name ________________________ Date ______________

Find any object that is approximately 100 grams. Then find 4 small objects. Find the mass of each object. Check the result with your partner's.

Measuring Mass Data Table

N Name of Object	1 Gram	5 Grams	10 Grams	20 Grams	*M* Total Mass (in ______ unit)

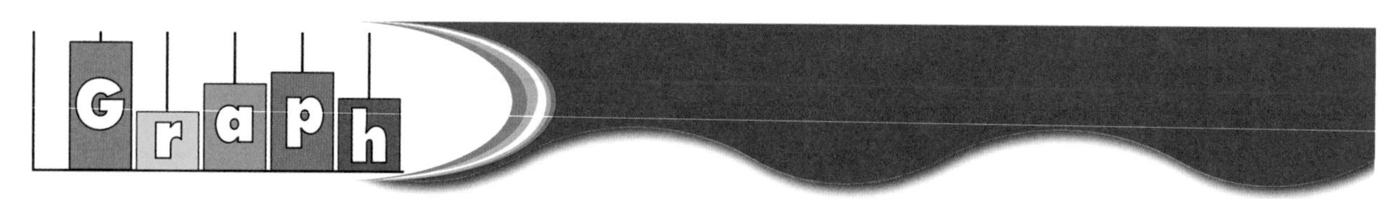

Make a bar graph of the data on graph paper. Label both axes.

Name ______________________ Date ____________

1. A. Which of your objects has the least mass?

____

B. If you had four of these objects, would their combined mass be more than 100 grams?

____

How did you figure it out?

____

____

____

2. A. Which of your objects has the most mass?

____

B. Would three 40-gram objects have more mass than your heaviest object?

____

How did you figure it out?

____

____

Name ______________________ Date ______________

3. **A.** Find the sum of the masses of your heaviest object and your lightest object.

____

B. Put these two objects in one balance pan. Find their total mass. Did you get the same answer as in Question 3A? Why or why not?

____

____

____

4.

[1] heaviest object [   ] lighter objects

How many of your lighter objects come closest to balancing your heaviest object? How do you know?

____

____

____

Name ______________________________ Date ________________

5. Bo uses these masses.

1 g	5 g	10 g	50 g
3	1	2	1

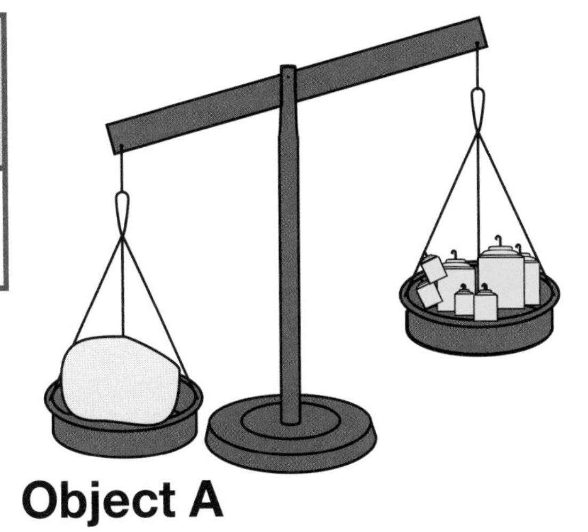

And the balance looks like this.

Then, Bo uses these masses.

1 g	5 g	10 g	50 g
4	1	2	1

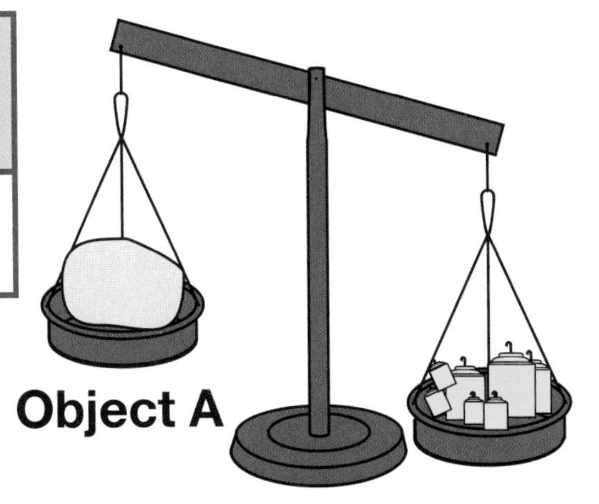

And the balance looks like this.

Estimate the mass of Object A. __________

Name ______________________ Date ______________

What's the Total Mass?

Homework

Dear Family Member:

Your child is learning to measure the mass of objects using a two-pan balance. He or she places the object in one pan. Standard masses are placed in the other pan until the two pans are balanced. Your child finds the total mass by adding up the values of the standard masses. Help your child complete the problems below.

Thank you for your help.

The picture shows the masses used to balance each object. What is the total mass of each object?

1. Eraser

   ____

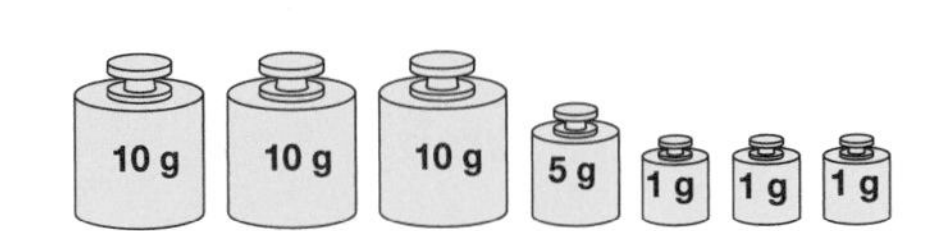

2. Meterstick

   ____

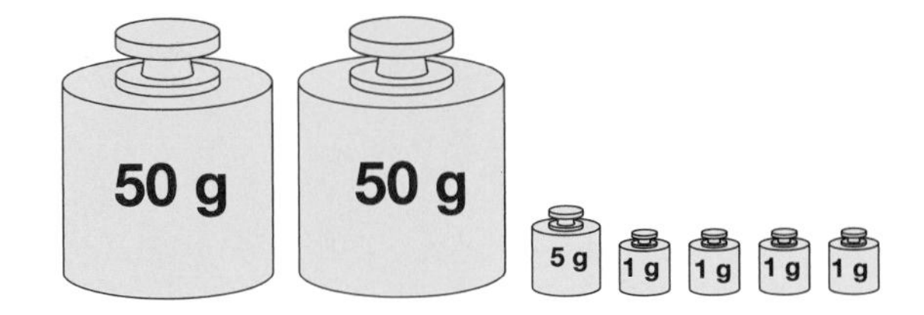

3. Three pieces of chalk

   ____

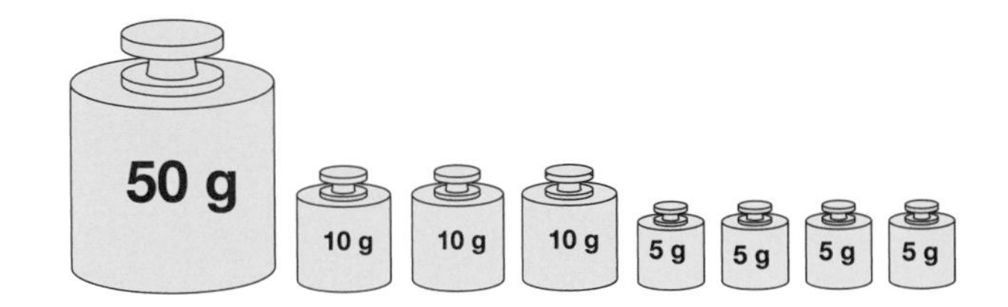

4. A sandwich

   ____

Unit 9

Ways of Adding Larger Numbers

	Student Guide	Adventure Book	Unit Resource Guide*
Lesson 1			
In the Ballpark	●		
Lesson 2			
An Addition Seminar	●		
Lesson 3			
The Nameless Scribe	●	●	
Lesson 4			
Exploring with Base-Ten Pieces	●		
Lesson 5			
Adding with Paper and Pencil	●		
Lesson 6			
Snack Shop Addition	●		

******Unit Resource Guide* **pages are from the teacher materials.**

Name ______________________ Date ______________

Price Cards

56¢	32¢	36¢	59¢
42¢	45¢	50¢	72¢
40¢	92¢	27¢	29¢
17¢	25¢	46¢	49¢
89¢	19¢	22¢	23¢

Name ______________________ Date ______________

Which Is Closer?

Katen and Tamika mixed up their price cards. They then pulled some to estimate. Circle the "could be" estimates, and cross out the "crazy" estimates. Give an estimate for the sum. Tell how you made your estimate. An example is done for you.

Example:

Katen pulled a 72¢, a 27¢, and a 36¢ card from the pile.

$1.50

$1.40

Estimate the sum. $1.25

I used quarters for my estimate. 75¢ + 25¢ + 25¢ = $1.25.

1. Tamika pulled a 32¢, a 29¢, and a 27¢ card from the pile.

   90¢ $1.50 60¢ $1.00 $2.00

Estimate the sum. ______

____

2. Katen and Tamika pulled a 56¢, a 32¢, a 72¢, and a 92¢ card from the pile.

   $1.00 $2.00 $4.00 $2.75 $2.50

Estimate the sum. ______

____

Name ______________________ Date ______________

Numbers and Sense

Solve the following problems by estimating the sum. Each time, tell how you made your estimate.

1. Katen and Arlene went to a baseball game. They counted baseball caps. Arlene counted 27 caps and then 14 caps. Katen counted 32 caps and 48 caps. Estimate the number of caps they counted in all.

   ____

   ____

2. The hot dog vendor sold 68 hot dogs with ketchup, 2 hot dogs with mustard, and 9 plain hot dogs. Estimate the number of hot dogs sold.

   ____

   ____

3. The Chicago Cubs and the Chicago White Sox played a doubleheader. The Cubs had 22 hits in the first game and 13 hits in the second. The White Sox had 28 hits in the first game and 17 hits in the second. Estimate the number of hits in all.

   ____

   ____

Name ______________________ Date ______________

Triangle Flash Cards: Group G

- **Cut out the flash cards. To practice an addition fact, cover the corner with the highest number. (It is shaded.) Add the two uncovered numbers.**
- **Divide the cards into three piles: those facts you know and can answer quickly, those you can figure out with a strategy, and those you need to learn.**
- **Practice the last two piles again. Then make a list of the facts you need to practice at home.**

Name _______________ Date _______________

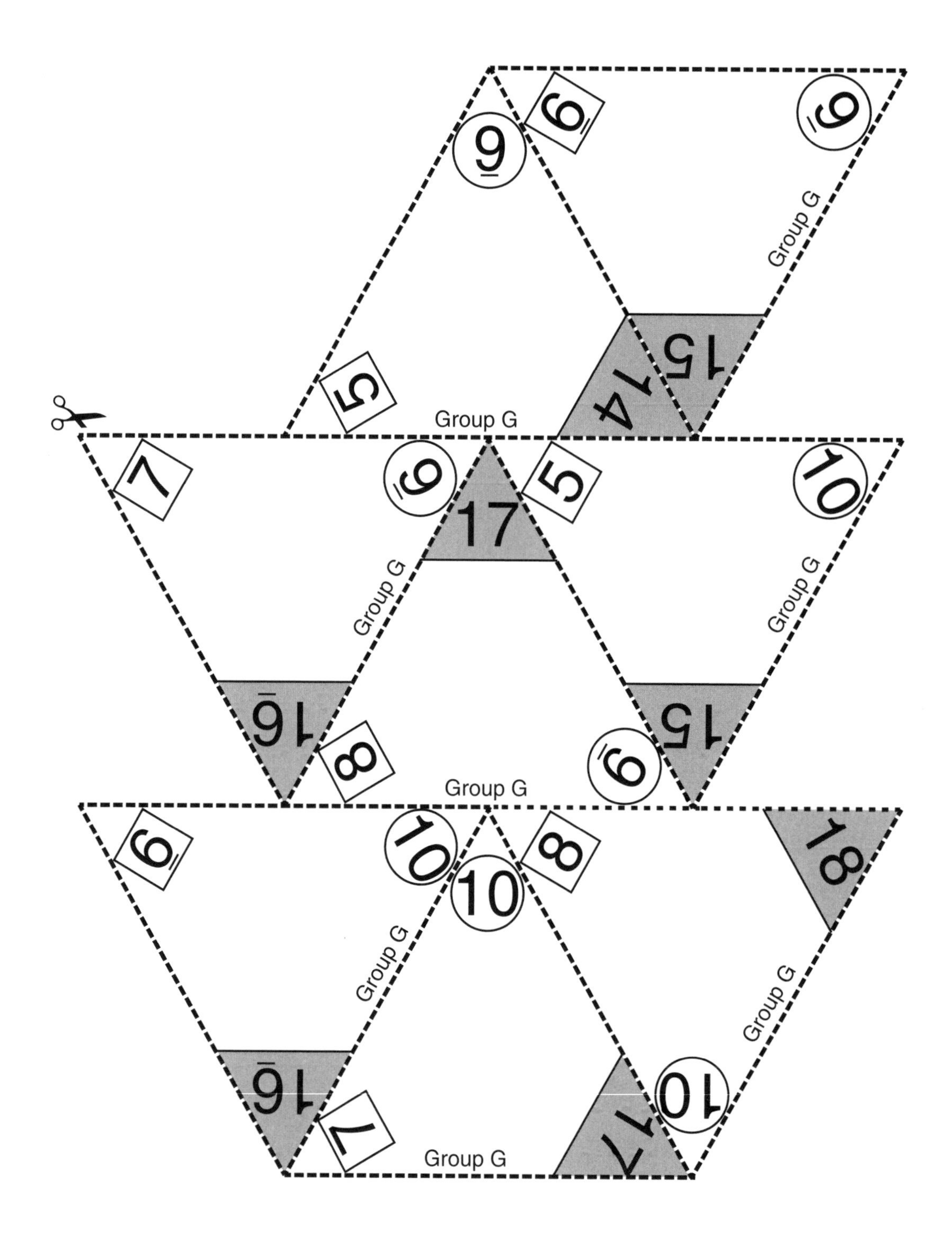

9
6
6
Group G
15
14
5
Group G
7
6
17
5
10
Group G
Group G
16
8
15
6
Group G
6
10
10
8
18
Group G
Group G
16
7
17
10
Group G

Name ______________________ Date ______________

Computer Game Seminar

The Compute-with-Us Game Company held a seminar for school children. The students talked about new computer games. Help total the data collected at the seminar. Explain your thinking for each problem. Use words and pictures.

1. Twenty-nine students were from Chicago, Illinois. Thirty-three students were from Springfield, Illinois. How many students came from Illinois?

____

____

____

2. In the morning session, the students named their favorite type of computer game. Fifty-five students liked sports games. Thirty-eight students liked space games. How many students were in the morning session?

____

____

____

Name ______________________ Date ____________

3. In the afternoon session, 54 students reported that space games were their favorite, 27 liked adventure games, and 32 liked sports games. Did more or less than 100 students attend the afternoon session?

____

____

____

4. In the morning session, 46 students drew new characters they would like to see in a game. In the afternoon session, 36 students drew new characters. How many students drew new characters?

____

____

____

5. Pretend you were at the seminar. What did you find out? Write a problem and find the answer.

____

____

____

Name ______________________ Date ______________

How Did They Do It?

Pretend you are a teacher. Check to see how your students solved this problem:

$$\begin{array}{r} 26 \\ +\ 58 \\ \hline \end{array}$$

Shanila showed her work like this:

$$\begin{array}{r} 26 \\ +58 \\ \hline 84 \end{array}$$

卌 卌 卌 卌 卌 |

卌 卌 卌 卌 卌 卌 卌 卌 卌 卌 卌 |||

What did she do to solve the problem?

Devon used the *200 Chart* and showed his work like this:

$$\begin{array}{r} 26 \\ +58 \\ \hline 84 \end{array}$$

26 36 46 56 66 76

77 78 79 80 81 82 83 84

What did he do?

On the back of this page, show another way to solve the problem.

Name ______________________ Date ______________

Acme Grocery Store

Dear Family Member:

Check that your child has chosen prices between 25¢ and 90¢ for the price tags. Ask your child to explain how he or she found the answer to each problem.

Thank you.

Fill in the blank price tags with prices between 25¢ and 90¢.

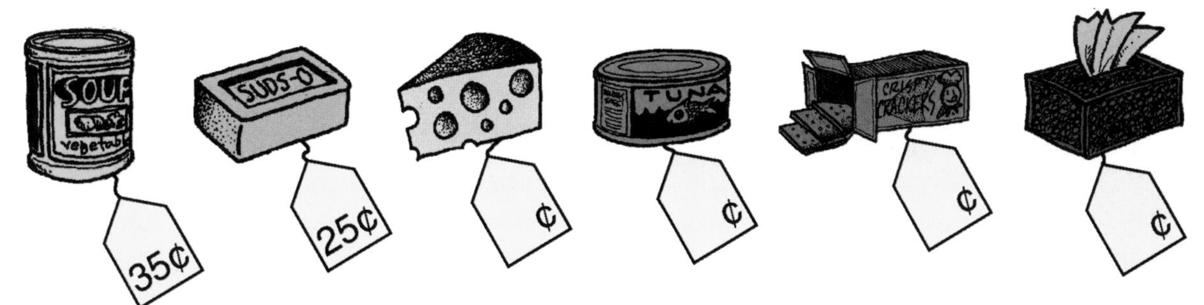

Find the total cost for each problem. Describe your thinking.

1. A can of soup and a bar of soap cost ____________.

____

____

2. A cheese wedge and a can of tuna cost ____________.

____

____

3. A box of crackers and a box of tissues cost ____________.

____

____

Name ______________________________ Date ______________

King Gupta's Feast

"We need one hundred fifty new golden plates, four hundred fifty flowers, three hundred one bananas, one hundred seventy cheeses, five hundred two sugar candies, and fifteen cakes," says King Gupta.

What should Krishna write down?

King Gupta requires ________ gold plates.	King Gupta requires ________ cheeses.
King Gupta requires ________ flowers.	King Gupta requires ________ candies.
King Gupta requires ________ bananas.	King Gupta requires ________ cakes.

Name ______________________ Date ______________

Building Addition Problems

Before you do the problems below, estimate the answer. Use base-ten pieces to solve each problem. Then explain how to do the problem another way.

1. The sum will be between ____ and ____.

$$\begin{array}{r} 15 \\ +\ 32 \\ \hline \end{array}$$

2. The sum will be between ____ and ____.

$$\begin{array}{r} 24 \\ +\ 58 \\ \hline \end{array}$$

3. The sum will be between ____ and ____.

$$\begin{array}{r} 65 \\ +\ 26 \\ \hline \end{array}$$

4. The sum will be between ____ and ____.

$$\begin{array}{r} 27 \\ 13 \\ +\ 55 \\ \hline \end{array}$$

Name ______________________ Date ______________

What Happened Here?

Michael completed the following problem:

$$\begin{array}{r} 48 \\ +\ 49 \\ \hline 817 \end{array}$$

1. Is this a reasonable answer for this problem? How do you know?

____

____

2. What do you think Michael might have done?

____

____

3. How would you solve this problem? Make sure you explain your thinking.

____

____

Name ______________________ Date ______________

Add to 100

Players

This is a game for two or more players.

Materials

- digit cards or regular playing cards
- paper
- pencil

(If you use the regular playing cards, use only the 1–9 cards.)

Rules

1. Deal out four cards to each player.
2. Each player uses the four cards to make an addition problem.
3. Each player solves his or her addition problem.
4. The player whose answer is closest to 100 takes everyone's cards and puts them aside.
5. Keep dealing four more cards to each player and making problems.
6. When all the cards are gone, the player who has collected the most cards wins.

Play several games. Then, write about what happened. Tell how you think you can win.

____

____

____

Name ______________________ Date ______________

Adding Two Ways

Solve the problem two ways. Show your thinking.

---

1. First way:

$$\begin{array}{r} 42 \\ +\ 49 \\ \hline \end{array}$$

---

2. Second way:

$$\begin{array}{r} 42 \\ +\ 49 \\ \hline \end{array}$$

Name ______________________ Date ______________

Think It Through

Homework

Solve the following problems using paper-and-pencil addition. Show your thinking.

1. Jenny and Jordan collect baseball cards. Jenny has 56 Chicago White Sox cards. Jordan has 48 Chicago Cubs cards. If they combine their collections, how many Chicago cards will they have?

2. Jenny was given 26 more White Sox cards to go with the 56 she already had. How many White Sox cards are now in her collection?

3. Jordan decided to collect Cardinal cards as well. He bought 35 cards to add to his collection of 48 cards. How many cards are now in his collection?

4. $\begin{array}{r} 25 \\ +\ 26 \\ \hline \end{array}$

5. $\begin{array}{r} 68 \\ +\ 23 \\ \hline \end{array}$

6. $\begin{array}{r} 45 \\ +\ 48 \\ \hline \end{array}$

7. $\begin{array}{r} 52 \\ +\ 47 \\ \hline \end{array}$

Name ______________________ Date ______________

Shooting Star Snack Shop Children's Menu

Food

Food	Price
Pizza Slice	79¢
Taco	59¢
Grilled Cheese Sandwich	89¢
Turkey Sandwich	99¢
Peanut Butter and Crackers	49¢
Bagel	29¢
Potato Chips	25¢
Pretzels	25¢
Brownie	35¢
Fruit Salad Cup	65¢
Carrot Sticks	29¢
Chicken Noodle Soup	55¢
Chili	75¢

Drinks	Small	Medium	Large
Milk	25¢	40¢	55¢
Lemonade	39¢	55¢	79¢
Orange Juice	55¢	70¢	85¢
Hot Chocolate	59¢	75¢	99¢

Name ______________________ Date ______________

Snack Shop Bills

Shooting Star Snack Shop
You have up to $5.00 to spend.

Customer's Name:

Enrique

Item	Price(¢)
Grilled Cheese	89¢
Carrot Sticks	29¢
Chicken Noodle Soup	55¢
Brownie	35¢
Large Milk	55¢

Total is between

________ and ________

Total ________

Is your total reasonable?

____

Shooting Star Snack Shop
You have up to ________ to spend.

Customer's Name:

____

Item	Price(¢)

Total is between

________ and ________

Total ________

Is your total reasonable?

____

Name ____________________ Date ____________

Shooting Star Snack Shop
You have up to $2.00 to spend.

Customer's Name: ____________

Item	Price(¢)
____________	______
____________	______
____________	______
____________	______
____________	______

Total is between ______ and ______

Total ______

Is your total reasonable? ____________

Shooting Star Snack Shop
You have up to $3.50 to spend.

Customer's Name: ____________

Item	Price(¢)
____________	______
____________	______
____________	______
____________	______
____________	______

Total is between ______ and ______

Total ______

Is your total reasonable? ____________

Name ______________________ Date ______________

Oops, I Spilled the Juice!

Splash Spiller and Nick bought lunch at the Shooting Star Snack Shop. Splash spilled juice on their bills. Some prices were blotted out.

Shooting Star Snack Shop Bill

Customer's Name Splash

Item	Price (¢)
Fruit Salad Cup	65¢
Pretzels	25¢
Cup of Applesauce	
Orange Juice	85¢
Total	$2.04

Shooting Star Snack Shop Bill

Customer's Name Nick

Item	Price (¢)
Chili	75¢
Taco	59¢
Banana Bread	
Medium Milk	40¢
Total	$2.23

How much did the applesauce cost?

How much did the banana bread cost?

Name ______________________ Date ____________

Snack Shop Carryout

Using your menu, make up your own problem on the bill below. If you ask others to place orders, you may use the space given to list more items. Show how you found your answer.

1.

Shooting Star Snack Shop		Customer's Name:
Item	Price(¢)	____________
____________	______	
____________	______	
____________	______	
____________	______	
____________	______	Is your total reasonable?
Total is between ______ and ______	Total ______	____________

Name ______________________ Date ____________

Use your menu to write the prices on each bill. Find the total in any way you choose. You may use a calculator.

2. **Shooting Star Snack Shop**

Customer's Name: ____________

Item	Price(¢)
Grilled Cheese	______
Potato Chips	______
Fruit Salad Cup	______
______	______
______	______

Total is between ______ and ______

Total ______

Is your total reasonable? ____________

3. **Shooting Star Snack Shop**

Customer's Name: ____________

Item	Price(¢)
Pizza Slice	______
Carrot Sticks	______
Lemonade	______
______	______
______	______

Total is between ______ and ______

Total ______

Is your total reasonable? ____________

Name ______________________ Date ______________

Many Ways to Solve a Problem

Solve the following problem two different ways. Use pictures and words to describe how you found the answer.

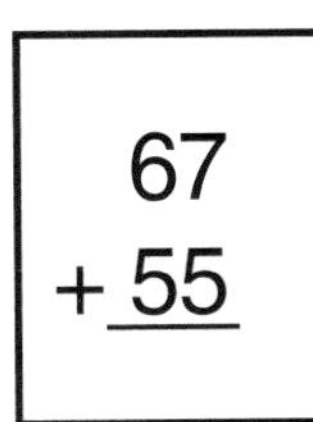

$$\begin{array}{r} 67 \\ +\ 55 \\ \hline \end{array}$$

First Way:

Second Way:

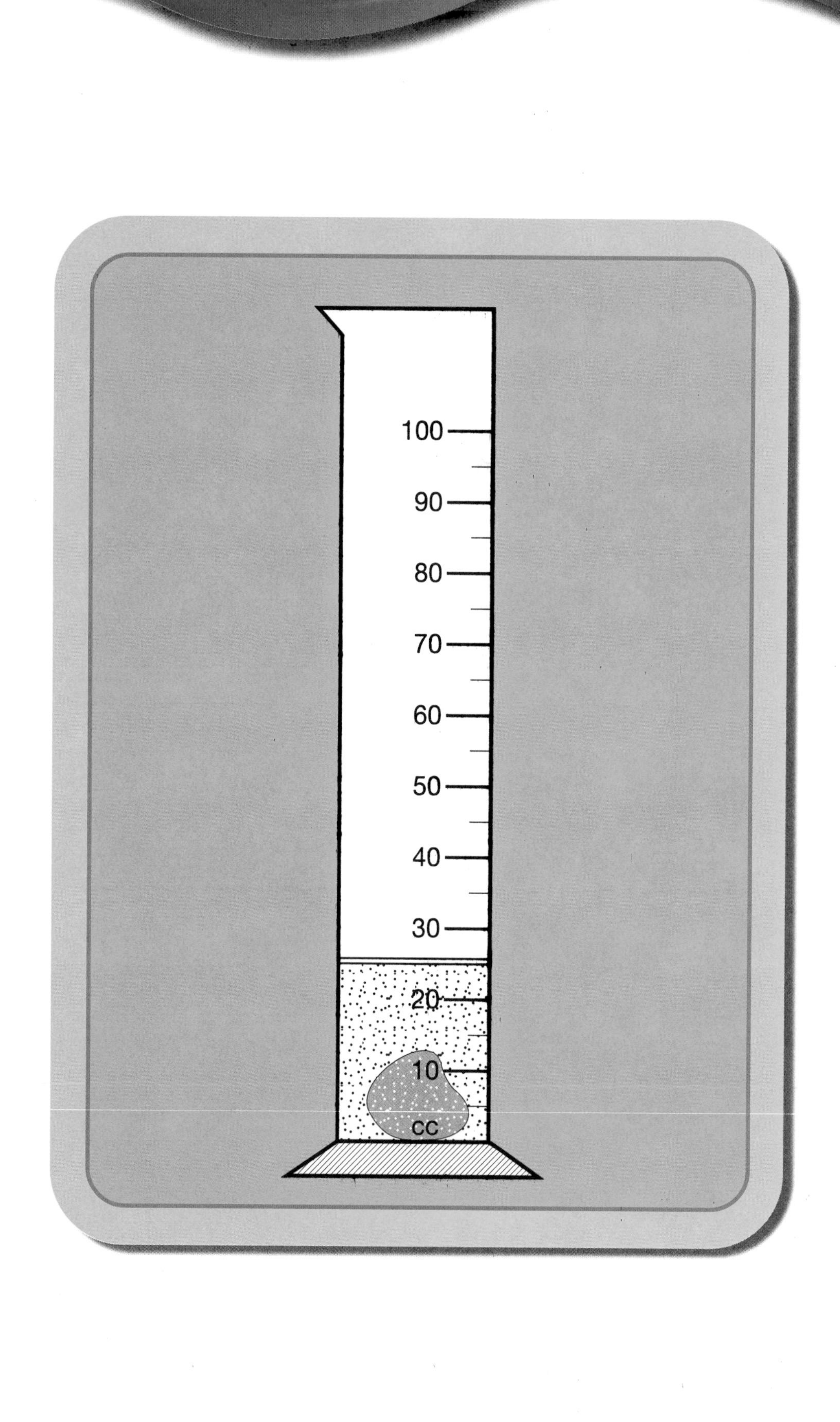
100
90
80
70
60
50
40
30
20
10
cc

Unit 10

Exploring Volume

	Student Guide	Adventure Book	Unit Resource Guide*
Lesson 1			
Reading Scales	●		
Lesson 2			
Reading Graduated Cylinders	●		
Lesson 3			
Filling Graduated Cylinders	●		
Lesson 4			
Measuring Volume	●		
Lesson 5			
Problem Solving with Volume	●		

******Unit Resource Guide*** **pages are from the teacher materials.**

Name ______________________ Date ______________

Scales Worksheet 1

Look at the scale to the right.

Write the number for each letter.

A. ________

B. ________

C. ________

D. ________

E. ________

F. ________

Find 85. Mark it G→.

Find 97. Mark it H→.

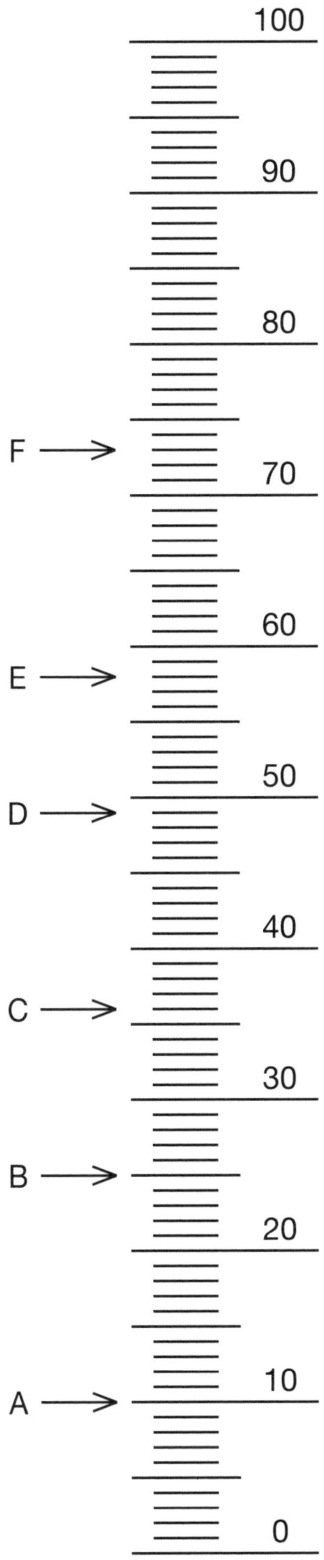

100
90
F →
80
70
60
E →
50
D →
40
C →
30
B →
20
A →
10
0

Name ______________________ Date ______________

Scales Worksheet 2

Look at the scale to the right.

Write the number for each letter.

A. ________

B. ________

C. ________

D. ________

E. ________

F. ________

Find 110. Mark it G→.

Find 119. Mark it H→.

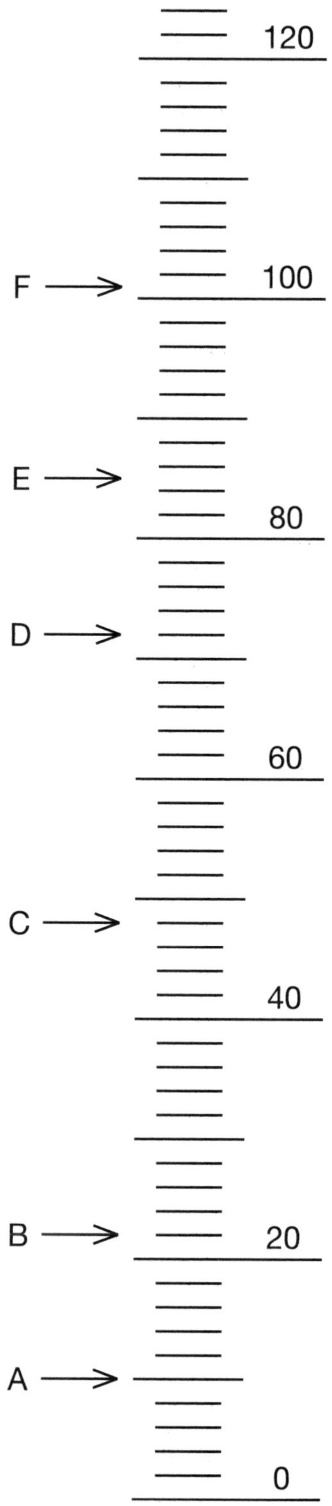

Name ______________________ Date ______________

Scales Worksheet 3

For problems 1 and 2, write the temperature the thermometer shows.

For problem 3, color the thermometer to show 85°. For problem 4, show 103°.

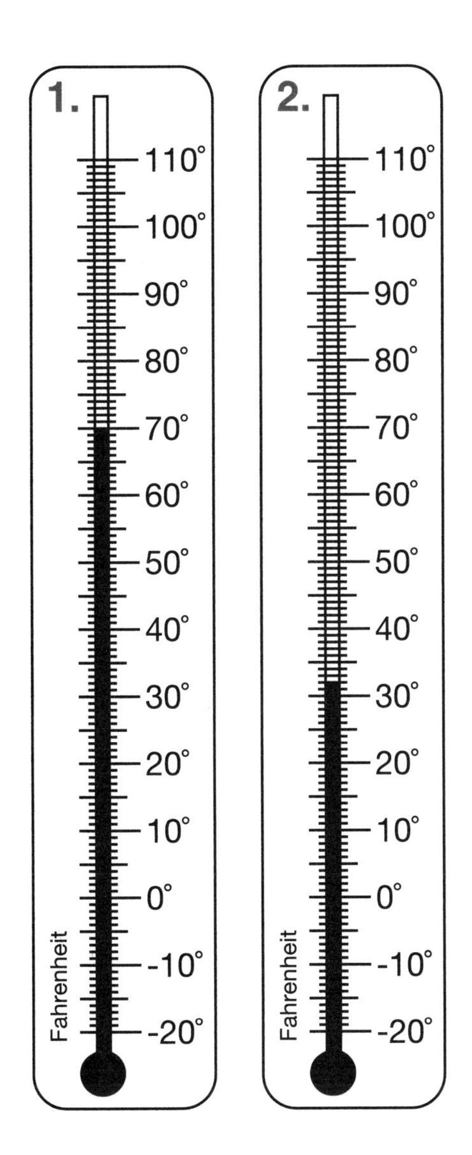

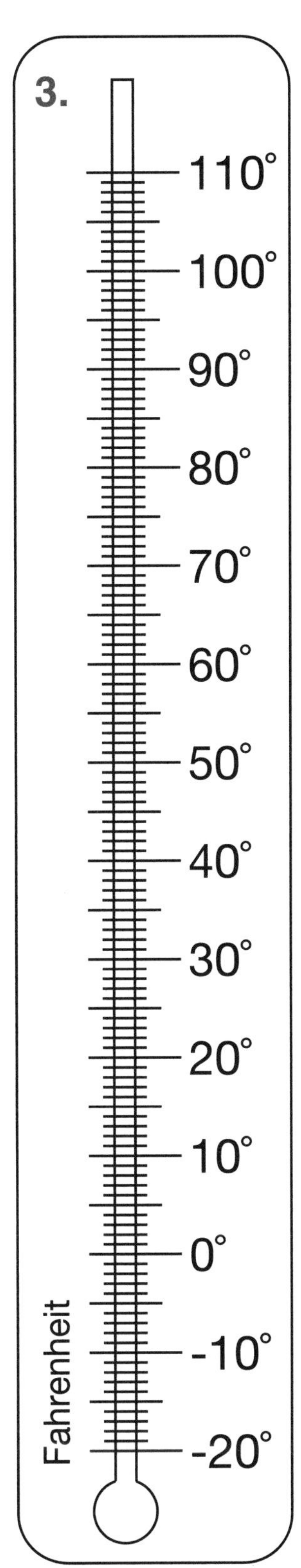

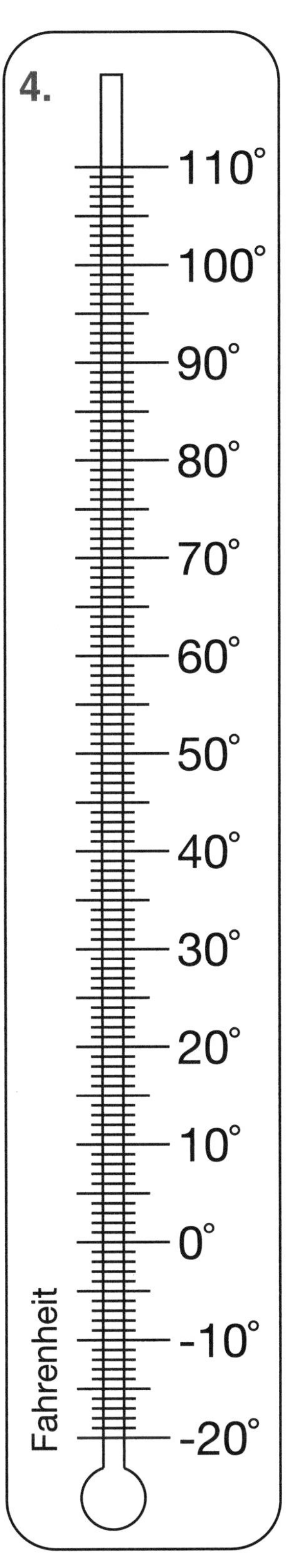

1. __________ **2.** __________

Name ______________________ Date ______________

Scales Worksheet 4

How fast is each car going?

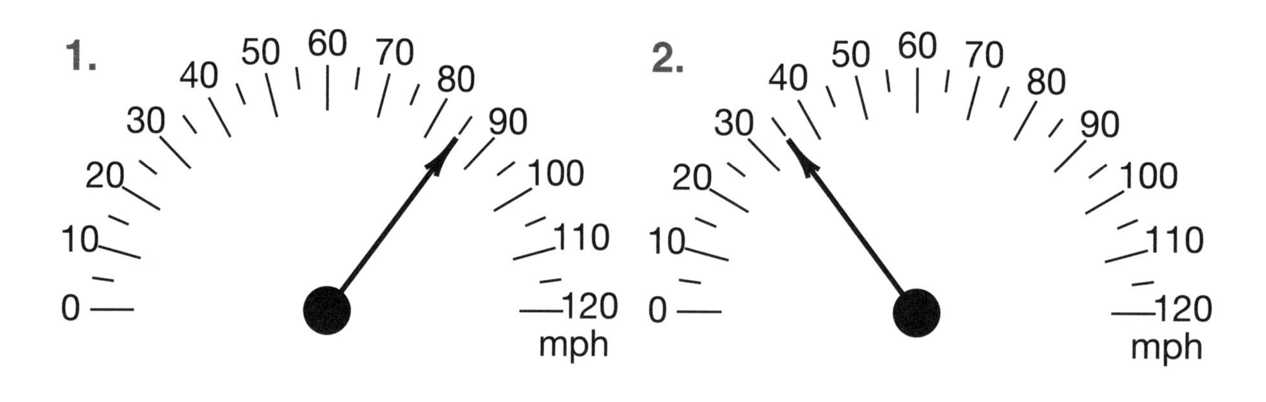

1. __________ 2. __________

Draw an arrow to show the speed on each speedometer.

3. 0 10 20 30 40 50 60 70 80 90 100 110 120 mph

80 mph

4. 0 10 20 30 40 50 60 70 80 90 100 110 120 mph

55 mph

Name ______________________ Date ______________

Scales at Home

Dear Family Member:

In class, we have been looking at examples of scales such as thermometers, metersticks, and so on. Please help your child as he or she looks around your home for other examples of scales.

Thank you.

Look around your home for examples of scales. These include control knobs for the oven, radio tuners, rulers, and so on. Draw a picture of three scales that you find. Include both the numbers and the units, if you can. Then write about each scale. Tell what it is and how it is used.

____

____

____

____

____

____

Name ______________________ Date ______________

Name ______________________ Date ______________

Understanding Scales

Look at the scale to the right.

Write the number for each letter.

A. __________

B. __________

C. __________

D. __________

E. __________

F. __________

Find 62. Mark it G→.

Find 75. Mark it H→.

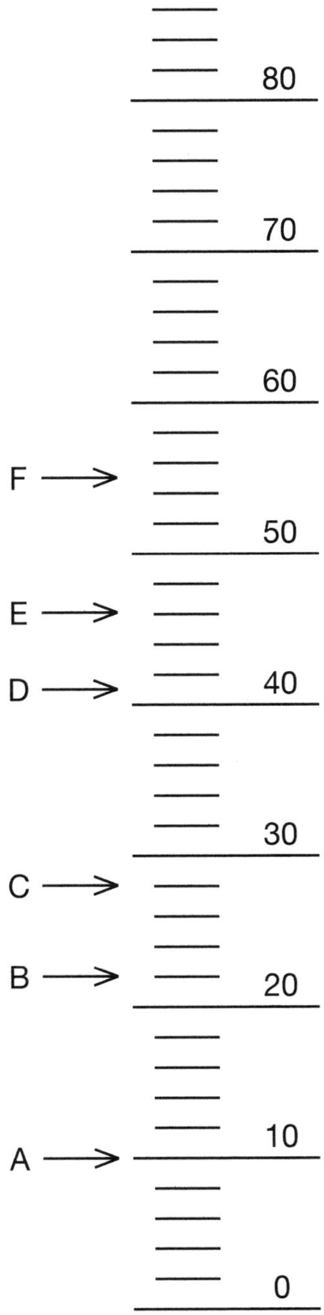

80

70

60

F →

50

E →

D → 40

30

C →

B → 20

10

A →

0

Name ______________________ Date ______________

Reading Graduated Cylinders

Work with a partner. Read the graduated cylinders your teacher has put around the room.

Cylinder	*V* Volume in ______ (*unit*)		
	Partner 1	Partner 2	Agreed Reading

Name ______________________________ Date ________________

Scales and Meniscus

Homework

Dear Family Member:

In class we have been learning how to measure the volume of an object or container. At home you measure volume using a measuring cup with a scale on it. In school we have been using a scientific tool called the graduated cylinder. When you measure using a glass or plastic measuring cup, you may have noticed that the water creeps up the sides of the cup a small amount. This is called the **meniscus**. To get an accurate reading, you have to read the line at the bottom of the meniscus.

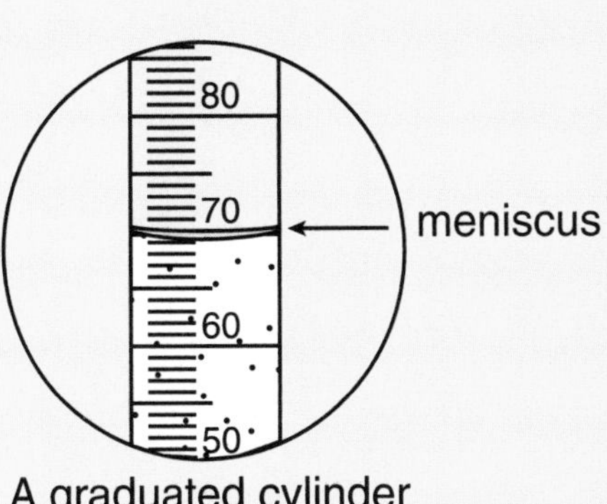

A graduated cylinder containing 69 cc.

You can help provide additional practice for your child by gathering various glass and plastic containers, including a measuring cup with a scale on it. If necessary, please help your child to fill these containers with water.

Thank you for your cooperation.

1. Fill some glass and plastic containers with water. Look at the water level in each container. Do you see a meniscus? Is it easier to see the meniscus in a glass container or a plastic container? Write about what happened.

____

____

____

____

____

Name ______________________ Date ______________

2. Find a measuring cup with a scale on it. What kind of scale is on the measuring cup? Draw a picture of the scale on the measuring cup. Then write about the scale. Explain how it is used.

Name ______________________ Date ______________

Reading a 2-Cup Measure

Look at the three pictures below. Each of the three children is trying to read the water level in the 2-cup measure. Explain the correct and incorrect methods you see.

Picture A: ______________________________

____

____

Picture B: ______________________________

____

____

Picture C: ______________________________

____

____

Name ______________________ Date ______________

Filling Graduated Cylinders

Work with a partner. Fill and read water levels in graduated cylinders.

Materials

- beaker filled with water
- eyedropper
- graduated cylinder
- paper towels (to clean up spills)

Directions

1. One partner names a target volume such as 50 cc or 75 cc.
2. The second partner pours water into the graduated cylinder to reach the target volume. Use the dropper to add a little extra water, if needed.
3. The first partner reads the volume and writes it down in the data table on the next page.
4. The second partner checks the reading and writes it down.
5. Both partners agree on the reading and record it.
6. After both partners agree, pour the water back into the beaker.
7. Repeat the process taking turns.

Name ______________________ Date ______________

First Partner's Reading	Second Partner's Reading	Agreed Reading

Name ______________________ Date ____________

How to Fill a Graduated Cylinder

Explain how to fill a graduated cylinder correctly. Use clue words like *first, next,* and *finally* to tell the steps in order.

____

____

____

____

____

____

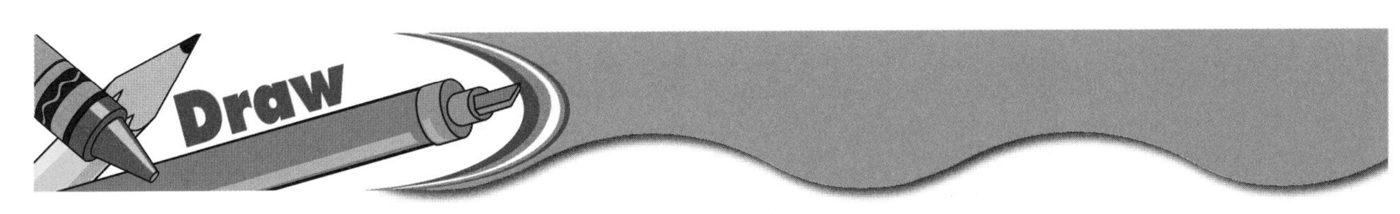

Draw a picture showing how to fill a graduated cylinder.

Name ______________________ Date ______________

Measuring Volume

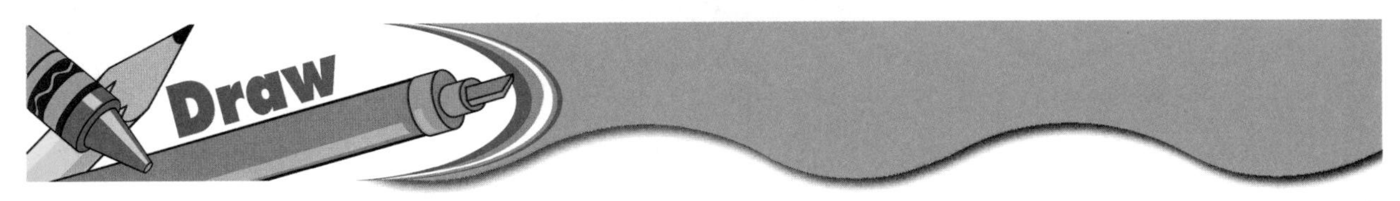

Draw a picture of the lab setup.

Name ______________________ Date ______________

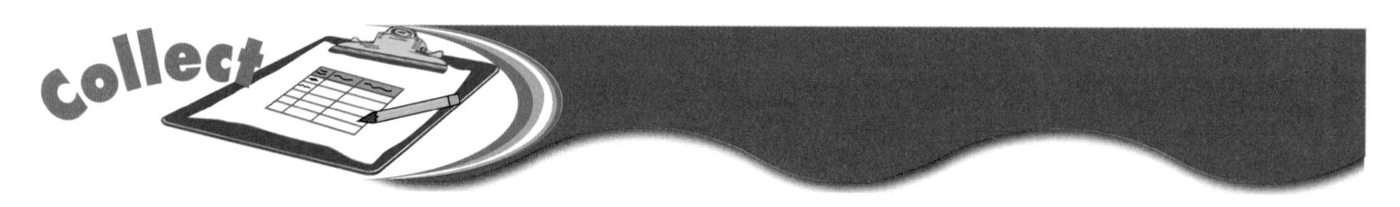

Fill a graduated cylinder with 80 cc of water. Pick at least four objects. One should be a chain of centimeter connecting cubes. Fill in the data table.

Measuring Volume Data Table 1

Object	*V* (Water) in ______ *unit*	*V* (Total) in ______ *unit*	*V* (Object) in ______ *unit*
chain of cm connecting cubes			

Name ______________________ Date ______________

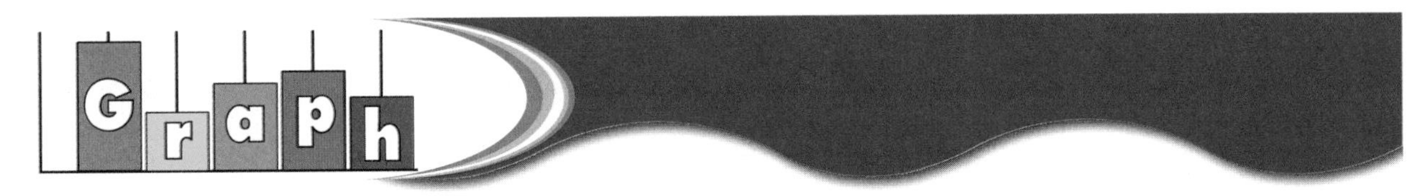

Make a bar graph of your data on a piece of bar graph paper.

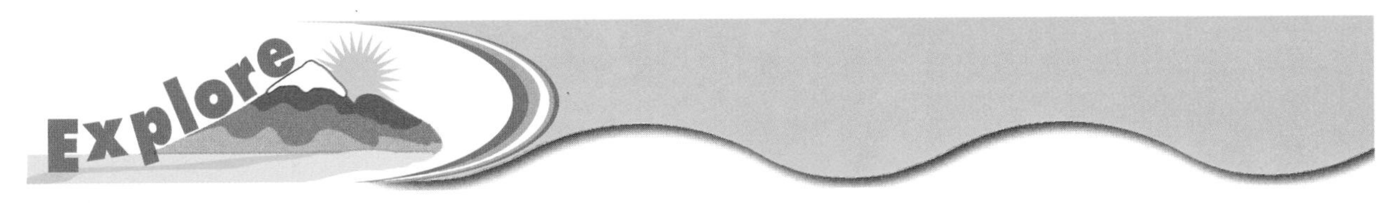

Work together to answer the following questions.

1. Which object has the most volume? What is its volume?

____

____

2. Which object has the least volume? What is its volume?

____

____

3. What is the difference in volume between the two objects? Show how you found your answer.

____

____

Name ______________________ Date ______________

4. Look at Measuring Volume Data Table 1. Find the volume of three times the number of objects listed in the first column. Suppose the water level starts at 80 cc. Which objects cause the water to overflow the 100 cc mark on the graduated cylinder?

Use Measuring Volume Data Table 2 to write your answers.

Measuring Volume Data Table 2

Object	*V* (Object) in ______ *unit*	*V* (triple) in ______ *unit*	Overflow 100 cc mark (Yes or No)

Name ______________________ Date ______________

How Many Will It Take to Overflow?

Homework

Dear Family Member:

Your child is measuring volume in class by finding the amount of water objects displace when they are submerged in a graduated cylinder. You can assist your child in conducting a related investigation at home. Gather the materials listed on this page. You may wish to supervise your child as he or she performs the experiment.

Thank you for your help.

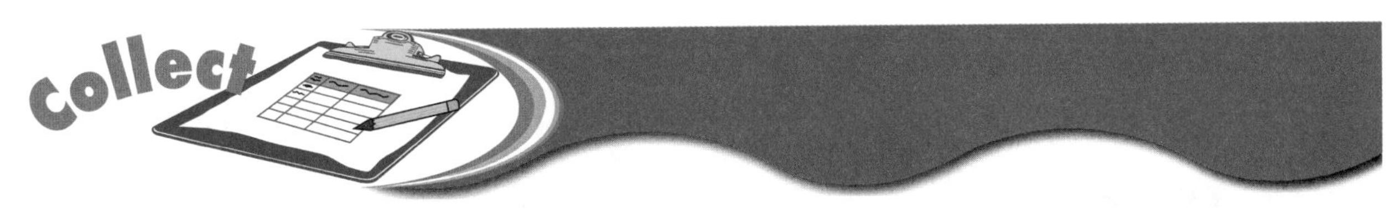

Ask an adult for help in choosing the materials listed below:

- 1 clear container (jar or glass)
- various objects, such as marbles, coins, nuts and bolts, and so on, that will sink and fit in the container (Don't choose very small objects.)
- tape or marker
- water
- paper towels

Name ______________________ Date ______________

Directions

1. Fill the container almost to the top with water.
2. Mark the level of the water with tape or a marker.
3. Estimate how many of the same type of object will make the water overflow the container.
4. Drop the objects carefully, one at a time, into the container. How many objects did it take to make the water level overflow?
5. Record the data you gather in the chart below.
6. Refill the container with water to the marked level. Drop another type of object.

Object	Estimated Number of Objects (to make the container overflow)	Actual Number of Objects (to make the container overflow)

Name ______________________ Date ______________

Volume Math Check

What is the volume of the clay in the cylinder labeled "after"? Write a number sentence to show how you got your answer.

____

____

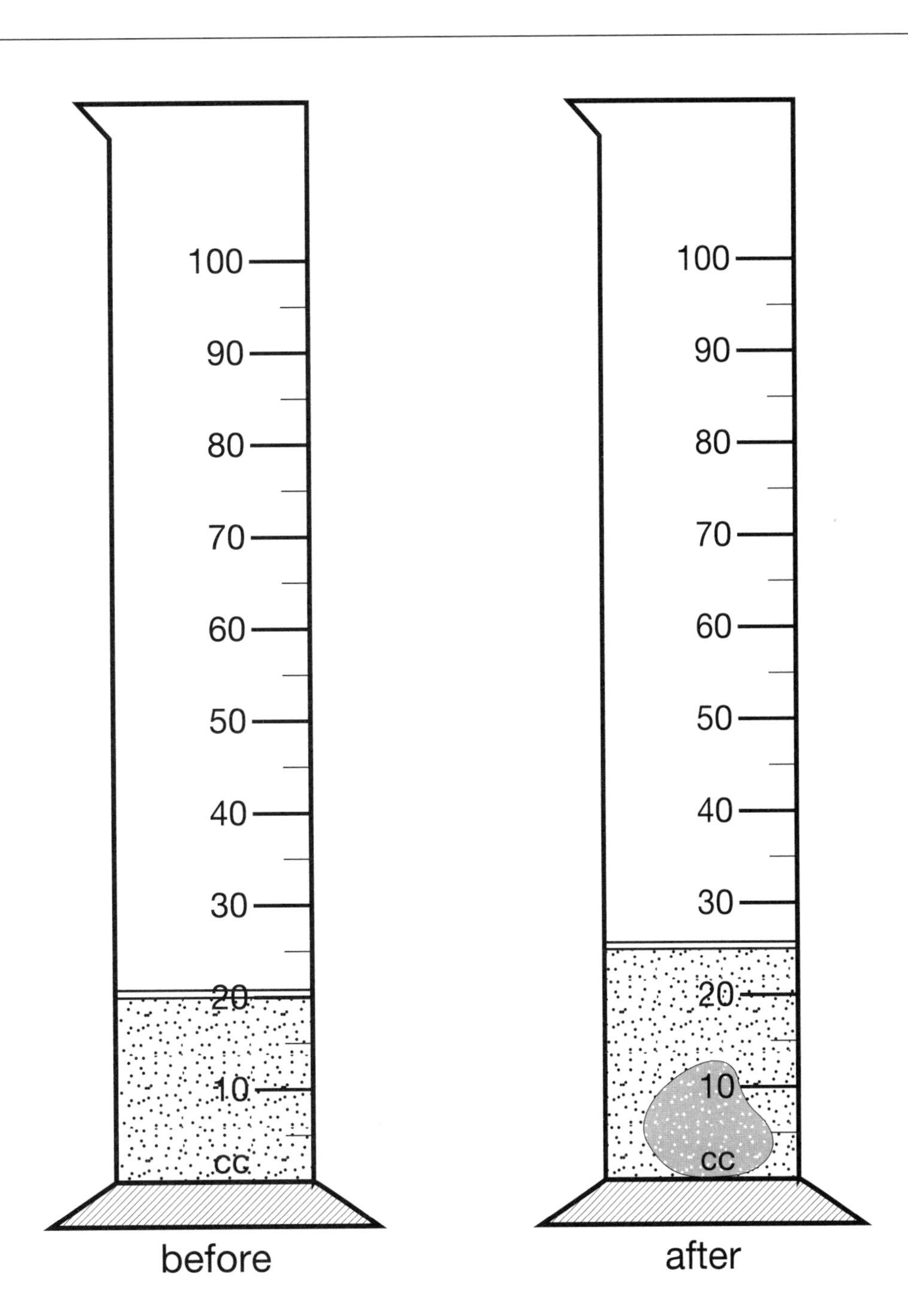

Name ______________________ Date ______________

Room for Ripley

In the book *Room for Ripley,* Carlos first put the castle into the bowl. Then he began adding the water. After the water was in the bowl, he added the fish.

What would happen if Carlos filled the bowl to the top with water and then tried to add the castle, plants, and fish? Explain. Talk about why it would happen.

Name ______________________ Date ____________

Volume Problem 1

Bill's rock has a volume of 25 cc. He put 50 cc of water into the graduated cylinder. What is the water level with both the object and the water in the cylinder? Show the water level. Shade the graduated cylinder with your pencil or crayon.

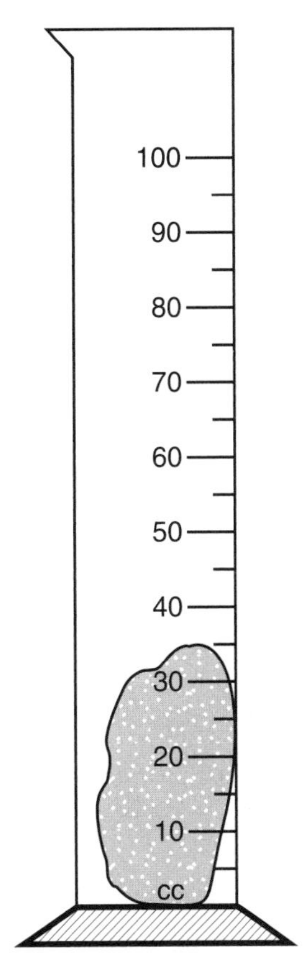

Explain how you got your answer.

____

____

____

____

Name ______________________ Date ____________

Volume Problem 2

Marlene has two objects. One object has a volume of 15 cc. The other object has a volume of 18 cc. She placed both objects in 60 cc of water.

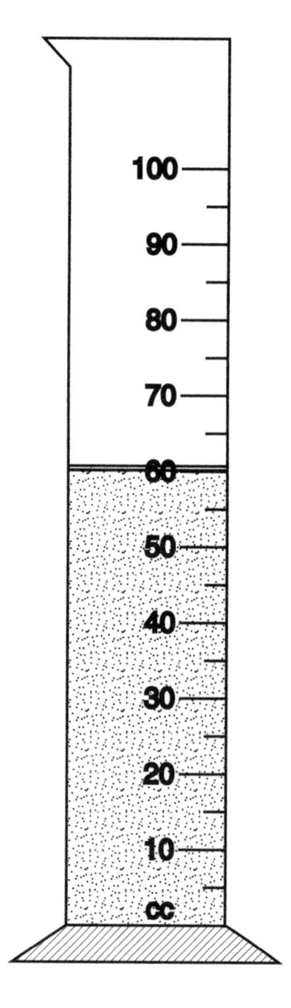

What will be the volume reading of the graduated cylinder? Write a number sentence to show how you got your answer.

____

____

Name ______________________________ Date ________________

Volume Problem 3

Jim put 40 cc of water into a graduated cylinder. He found the volume of Object A to be 6 cc. The volume reading with both objects in the graduated cylinder is 65 cc. Jim said, "I can figure out the volume of Object B without taking Object A out."

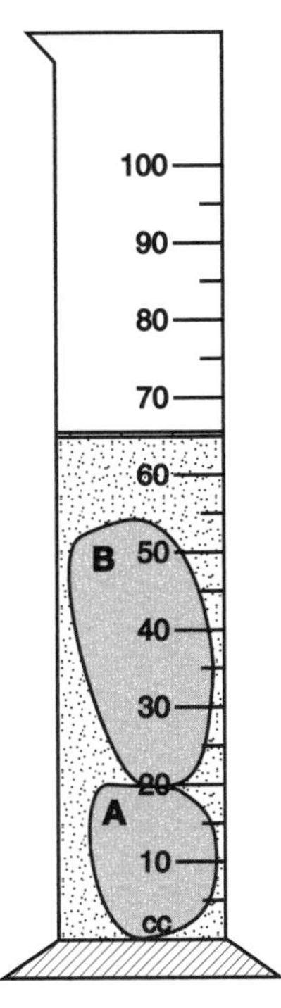

What is the volume of Object B? Use number sentences to help explain how you got your answer.

____

____

____

____

____

Name ______________________ Date ______________

Clayton's Volume Problem

Homework

Dear Family Member:

Your child is learning to read volumes on graduated cylinders. Help your child complete the problem below.

Thank you.

Clayton put 12 centimeter connecting cubes into water. The graduated cylinder reads 72 cc.

How much water is in the graduated cylinder? Write a number sentence to show how you got your answer.

____

____

____

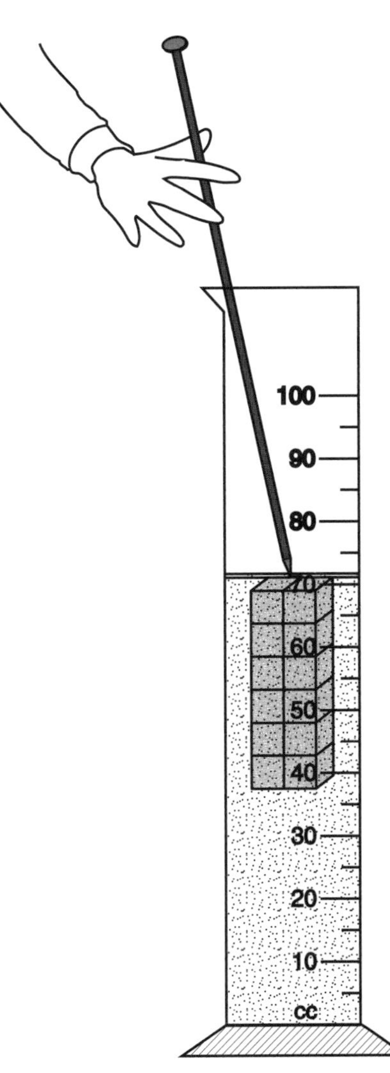

Glossary

This glossary provides definitions or examples of key terms in the Grade 2 lessons as a resource for students and parents. See the Glossary in the *Teacher Implementation Guide* for more detailed definitions.

A

Area (Unit 16)
The amount of space a shape covers. Area is measured in square units.

B

Base-ten Pieces (Unit 6)
A set of blocks that students use to represent numbers. A skinny is made of 10 bits and a flat is made of 100 bits.

Nickname	Picture
bit	
skinny	
flat	

Bit (Unit 6)
The smallest of the base-ten pieces. It often represents 1. (See also base-ten pieces.)

C

Centimeter (Unit 5)
A unit of length in the metric system. A centimeter (cm) is 1/100 of a meter. This rectangle is one centimeter long.

Cone (Unit 17)
A type of three-dimensional shape. Examples:

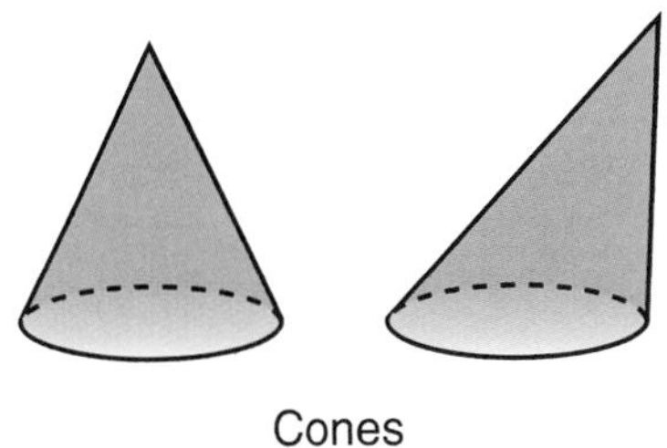

Cones

Corner (Unit 15)
A corner is the point where two sides or edges of a shape meet. Also called a vertex.

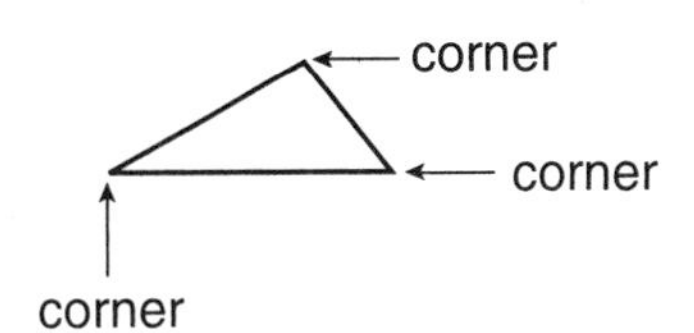

Cube (Unit 17)
A three-dimensional shape with six square faces that are all the same size.

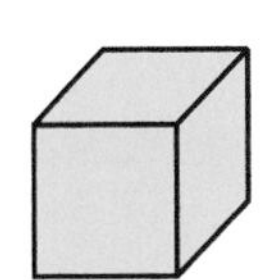

Cube Model (Unit 7)
A shape made with connecting cubes.

Cube Model Plan (Unit 7)
A grid that shows how to build a cube model. The number in each square shows the number of cubes stacked over that square.

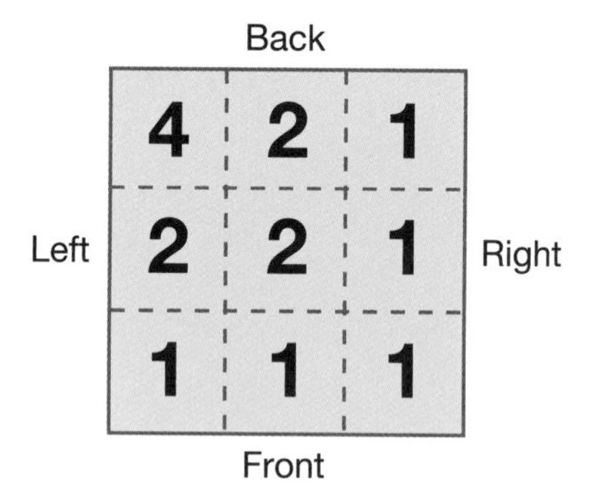

See the picture of the cube model for this plan under Cube Model.

Cubic Centimeter (Unit 10)
The volume of a cube that is one centimeter long on each edge.

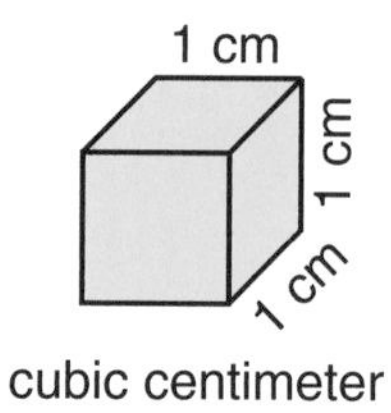

Cubit (Unit 4)
A very old unit of length. It is the distance from the elbow to the tip of the longest finger.

Cylinder (Unit 15)
A type of three-dimensional shape. Examples:

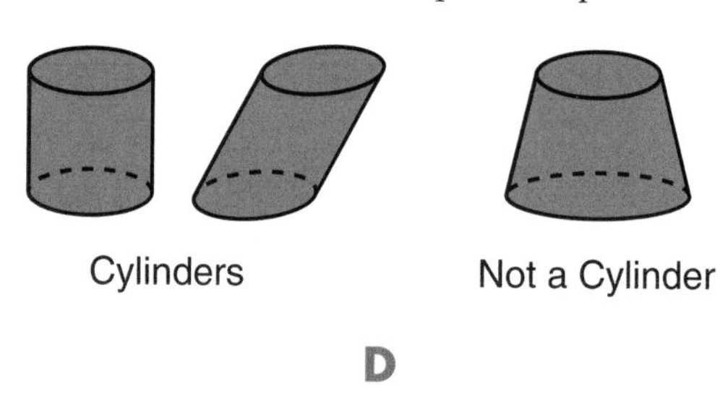

D

E

Edge (Unit 17)
A line where two faces of a three-dimensional shape meet.

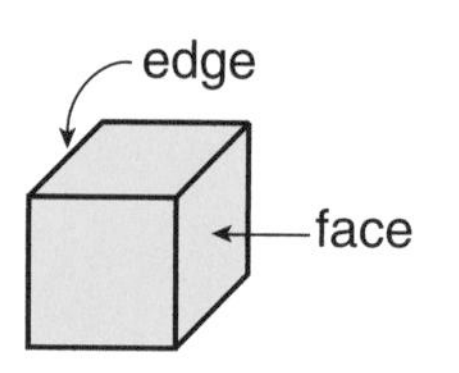

Equal-arm Balance (Unit 8)
See two-pan balance

Estimate (Unit 4)
1. (adjective) a number that is close to the desired number
2. (verb) to approximate

Even Number (Unit 2)
Numbers that are doubles. The numbers 0, 2, 4, 6, 8, 10, etc., are even. The number 28 is even because it is 14 + 14.

F

Face (Unit 17)
A two-dimensional shape that is one side of a three-dimensional shape.

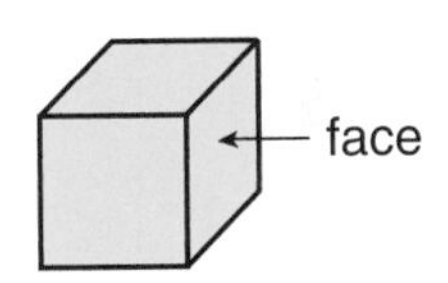

Fact Families (Unit 11)
Related math facts. These four number sentences are a fact family:
$1 + 2 = 3$
$2 + 1 = 3$
$3 - 2 = 1$
$3 - 1 = 2$

Flat (Unit 6)
A block that is one of the base-ten pieces. A flat is made of 100 bits. It often represents 100. (See also base-ten pieces.)

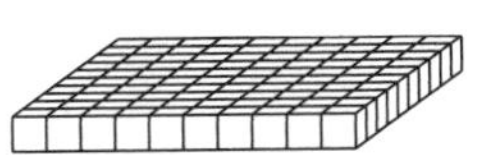

Flip (Unit 15)
A way of moving a two-dimensional shape. These dotted triangles are flipped over the lines.

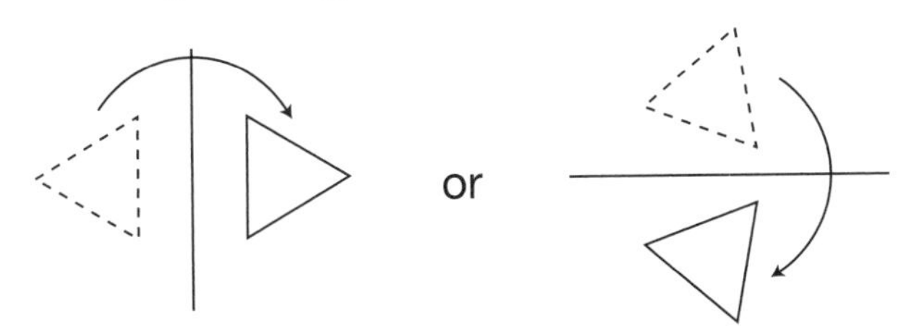

Function Machine (Unit 19)
A "machine" that follows a rule. It gives exactly one output number for any input number. This is a data table for an "Add 2" machine.

Input	Output
0	2
1	3
5	7
18	20

G

Gram (Unit 8)
The basic unit used to measure mass in the metric system. An ounce is about 28 grams. One gram is about the mass of a raisin.

H

Hand Span (Unit 4)
The distance from the tip of your thumb to the tip of your baby finger with your hand spread as wide as possible.

Horizontal Axis (Unit 2)
In a coordinate grid, the left/right axis.

I

Interval (Unit 2 & Unit 5)
All the numbers between (and including) two numbers.

J

K

L

Leftover (Unit 12 & Unit 19)
A number that remains or is left in a problem about equal sharing.

Line Symmetry (Unit 15)
A shape has line symmetry if it can be folded into two matching halves.

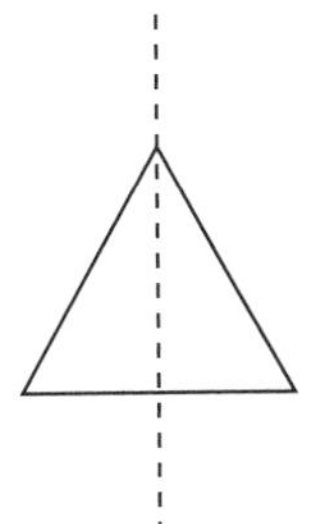

This shape has line symmetry.

This shape does not have line symmetry.

Line of Symmetry (Unit 15)
A line through a shape. If you fold the shape along this line, then one half of the figure matches the other.

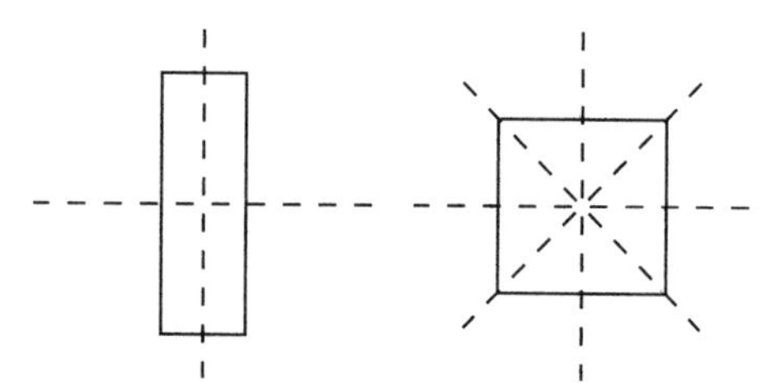

The dotted lines are lines of symmetry.

M

Mass (Unit 8 & Unit 10)
Mass is the amount of matter in an object. Metric units for mass are grams and kilograms. An object with a mass of one kilogram has a weight of about 2.2 pounds (on Earth). The mass of an object is the same everywhere, but its weight may vary. For example, if an object has a mass of 1 kilogram on Earth, it would have a mass of 1 kilogram on the moon, but it would weigh only one-sixth as much as it does on Earth.

Median (Unit 5)
The number "in the middle" of a set of data. Example: Jonah rolled a car down a ramp three times. The first time it rolled 30 cm. The second time it rolled 28 cm. The third time it rolled 33 cm. He put the numbers in order: 28 cm, 30 cm, 33 cm. 30 cm is the median because it is in the "middle" of his data.

Meniscus (Unit 10)
The curved surface formed when a liquid creeps up the side of a graduated cylinder.

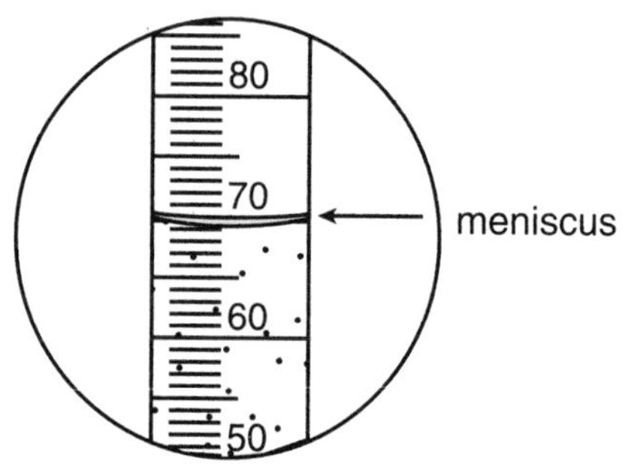

A graduated cylinder containing 69 cc.

Meter (Unit 5)
A unit of length in the metric system. A meter is a bit more that 39 inches.

Mr. Origin (also Ms. Origin) (Unit 18)
A plastic figure that helps children learn about direction and distance. Mr. Origin has a mitten on his right hand and a button on his front.

Multiplication Number Sentence (Unit 12)
A number sentence uses numbers and symbols instead of words to describe a problem. A multiplication number sentence describes a multiplication problem. For example, a multiplication number sentence for the problem "5 birds landed on a branch. Each bird had two seeds. How many seeds do all 5 birds have?" is $5 \times 2 = 10$.

N

Number Sentence (Unit 12)
A number sentence uses numbers and symbols instead of words to describe a problem. For example, a number sentence for the problem "5 birds landed on a branch. Two more birds also landed on the branch. How many birds are on the branch?" is $5 + 2 = 7$.

O

Odd Number (Unit 2)
A number that is not even. The odd numbers are 1, 3, 5, 7, 9, and so on.

P

Parallel Lines (Unit 15)
Lines that do not meet. Lines that are always the same distance apart.

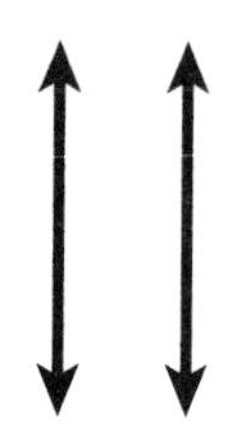

Perimeter (Unit 20)
The distance around a two-dimensional shape.

Place Value (Unit 6)
The value of a digit in a number. For example, the 5 is in the hundreds place in 4573, so it stands for 500.

Prism (Unit 17)
A type of 3-dimensional shape. Examples:

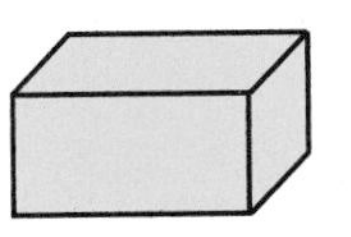
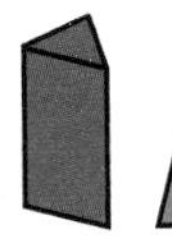

Prisms

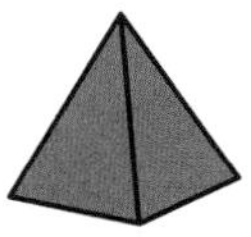

Not a Prism

Pyramid (Unit 17)
A type of 3-dimensional shape. Examples:

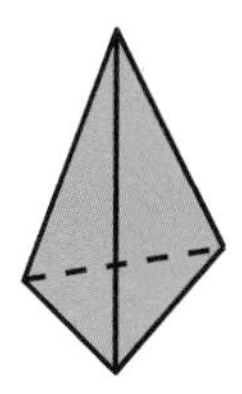

Triangular pyramid

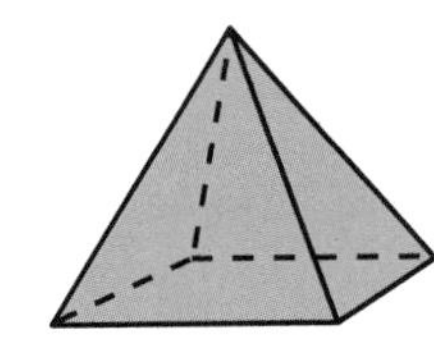

Rectangular pyramid

Rectangle (Unit 15)
A shape with four sides and with four square corners.

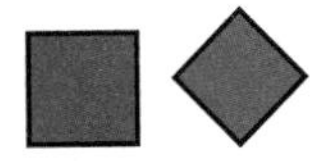

Rectangles

Not a Rectangle

Rectangular Prism (Unit 17)
A prism whose faces are all rectangles.

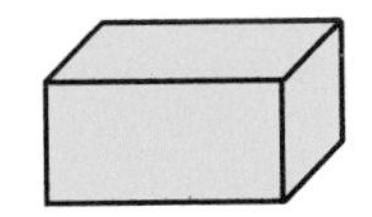

Rectangular prism

Rectangular Pyramid (Unit 17)
A pyramid with a rectangle for a base.

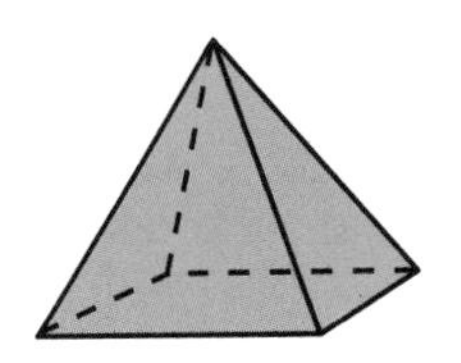

Rectangular pyramid

Reflection (Unit 15)
See flip.

Related Facts (Unit 11)
Fact families. For example, these facts are related:
$1 + 2 = 3$
$2 + 1 = 3$
$3 - 2 = 1$
$3 - 1 = 2$

Remainder (Unit 12)
A number that remains or is left after a division problem.

Rotation (Unit 15)
See turn.

Rotational Symmetry (Unit 15)
See turn symmetry.

S

Sample (Unit 13)
A smaller group taken out of a large collection.

Skinny (Unit 6)
A block that is one of the base-ten pieces. It is made of 10 bits. It often represents 10. (See also base-ten pieces.)

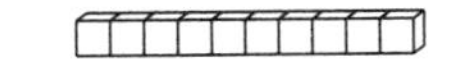

Slide (Unit 15)
A way of moving a two-dimensional shape. It moves a shape a certain distance in a certain direction.

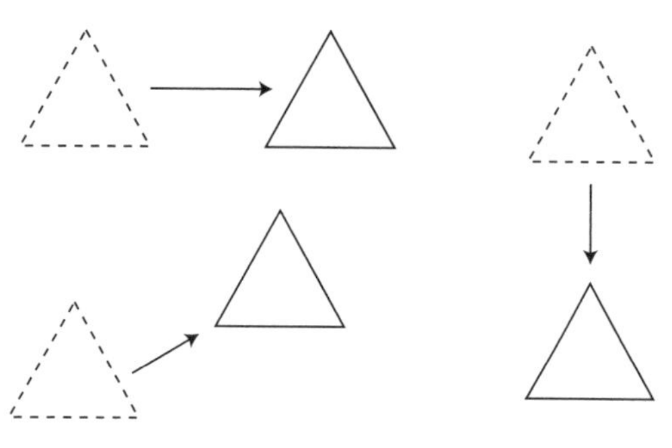

Sliding a triangle

Sphere (Unit 17)
A type of three-dimensional shape. A basketball is a common object shaped like a sphere.

Square (Unit 4 & Unit 15)
A rectangle that has four sides of equal length.

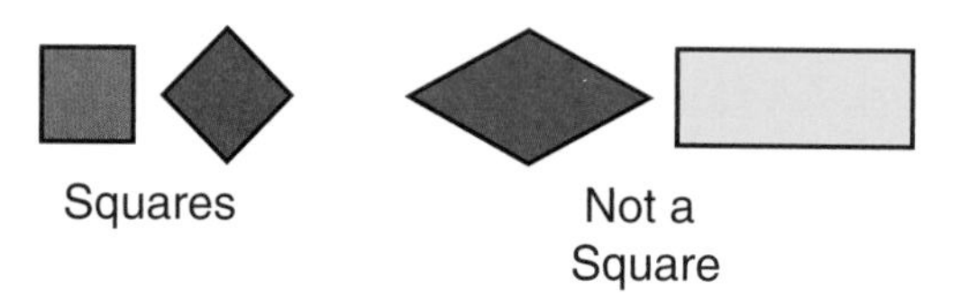

Square Centimeter (sq cm) (Unit 16)
The area of a square that is 1 cm long on each side.

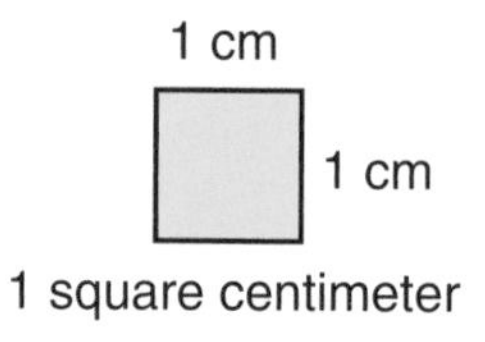

1 square centimeter

Standard Unit of Measure (Unit 5)
Universally accepted quantities used in measuring variables, e.g., centimeters and inches are standard units used to measure length and square centimeters and square inches are used to measure area.

Sum (Unit 3)
The answer to an addition problem.

Survey (Unit 19)
An investigation carried out by collecting data and then analyzing it.

T

Tally Marks (Unit 2)
A way to record a count by making marks.
Tallies are usually grouped in fives, 卌|||.

Translation (Unit 15)
See slide.

Trapezoid (Unit 15)
A four-sided shape with exactly one pair of parallel sides.

Triangular Prism (Unit 17)
A prism with a triangular base.

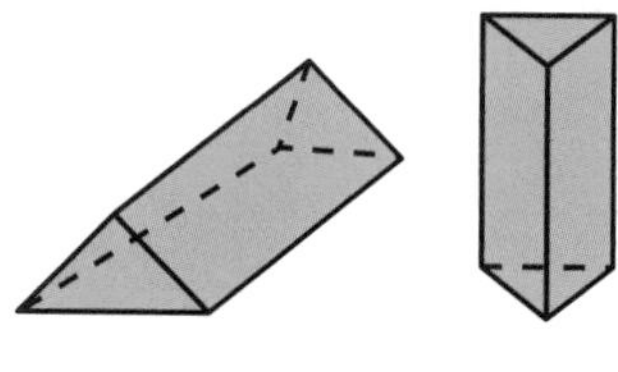

Triangular prisms

Triangular Pyramid (Unit 17)
A pyramid with a triangular base.

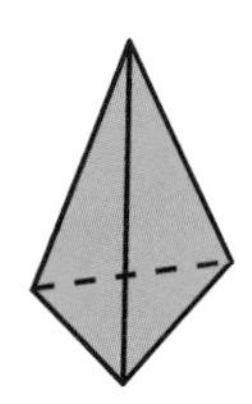

Triangular pyramid

Turn (Unit 15)
A way of moving a two-dimensional shape. A turn moves a shape around a point in its center.

Triangle before and after half turn.

Turn Symmetry (Unit 15)
A shape has turn symmetry if you can turn it around a point in its center so that it "fits" itself. For example, a square has turn symmetry.

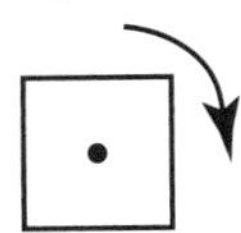

Two-dimensional Shapes (Unit 17)
Flat shapes.

Two-pan Balance (Unit 8)
A device for measuring mass that works by balancing an object against standard masses. Also called an equal-arm balance.

U

Unit (of Measurement) (Unit 10 & Unit 16)
A fixed amount used to measure. For example, centimeter, foot, kilogram, and quart are units of measurement.

Value (Unit 13)
The possible outcomes of a variable. For example, red, green, and blue are possible values for the variable *color.* Two meters and 6 inches are possible values for the variable *length.*

Variable (Unit 4 & Unit 13)
Something that changes or varies in an investigation.

Vertex (Unit 17)
See corner.

Volume (Unit 6, Unit 7 & Unit 10)
The measure of the amount of space occupied by an object. Volume is measured in cubic units.

Weight (Unit 8 & Unit 10)
Weight is a measure of the pull of gravity on an object. In the U.S. weight is usually measured in the English system that uses ounces and pounds as units of measure. If an object has a weight of 1 pound on Earth, it would have a weight of 1/6 pound on the moon, even though it would have the same mass as it does on Earth.

Width (of a rectangle) (Unit 16)
The distance along one side of a rectangle is the length and the distance along an adjacent side is the width.

Z

Index

The index provides page references for the *Student Guide.* Definition or explanation of key terms can be found in the glossary. A good source for information on the location of topics in the curriculum is the *Scope and Sequence* in Section 5 of the *Teacher Implementation Guide.*

K

O

S

T

U

V

W

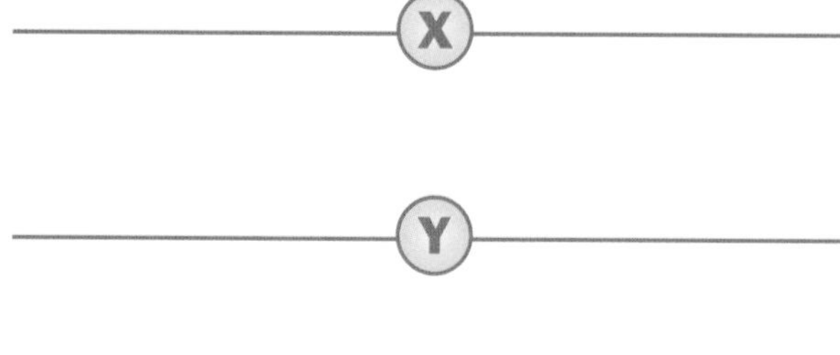

X

Y

Z